1001 IDEAS FOR
DECKS

CREATIVE
HOMEOWNER®

1001 IDEAS FOR
DECKS

Joe Provey

CREATIVE HOMEOWNER®, Upper Saddle River, New Jersey

1001 Ideas for Decks
Produced by: Home & Garden Editorial Services
Author: Joe Provey
Layout and Copyediting: Jill Potvin Schoff
Copyeditor: Owen Lockwood
Editorial Assistants: Briana Porco, MaryAnn Kopp
Photo Prepress: Carl Weese
Illustrations: Bob La Pointe
Front Cover Photography: courtesy of TimberTech;
insets courtesy of *top to bottom* Highpoint Deck Lighting; TimberTech; Wolman
Back Cover Photography: *top left* courtesy of TimberTech;
bottom left courtesy of Universal Forest Products; *top middle* courtesy of
Weyerhaeuser; *bottom middle* Robert LaPointe;
top right courtesy of Trex; *bottom right* courtesy of Western
Red Cedar Lumber Association www.wrcla.org

Creative Homeowner
VP/Editorial Director: Timothy O. Bakke
Production Manager: Kimberly H. Vivas
Art Director: David Geer
Managing Editor: Fran Donegan
Editorial Assistants: Nora Grace, Jennifer Calvert
Plans Layout: Maureen Mulligan

1001 Ideas for Decks, First Edition
Library of Congress Control Number: 2006931868
ISBN-10: 1-58011-333-8
ISBN-13: 978-1-58011-333-5

Current Printing (last digit)
10 9 8 7 6 5 4 3

CREATIVE HOMEOWNER®
A Division of Federal Marketing Corp.
24 Park Way
Upper Saddle River, NJ 07458
www.creativehomeowner.com

Dedication

To my mom, Dorothy, for teaching me to see, and to my dad, Joe, for teaching me to persevere.

Acknowledgments

We would like to thank the many architects, photographers, and decking product manufacturers that made this book possible. Special thanks to illustrator Bob La Pointe, to photographers Brian Vanden Brink and Robert Perron, to the California Redwood Association, and to the Western Red Cedar Lumber Association.

Contents

Introduction

Decks are the least expensive way to add square feet to your living space. They are relatively straightforward to build and don't require elaborate foundations, and adding one won't interfere with your day-to-day routine nearly as much as a kitchen remodeling. Because of their simplicity, however, many homeowners and builders don't stop to consider all the possibilities that decks can offer. With a little forethought, they can be a lot more than rectangles with guardrails.

Designing a deck, long thought of as tacking a platform to the back of the house, involves choices of height, shape, style, color, lighting, materials, and accessories. The right decisions make this raised deck a perfect place for taking in the sunset.

Decks can be places to cook and entertain, soak in a spa, gaze into a fire, exercise a green thumb, or sunbathe. They can be made comfortable—with protection from sun, wind, rain, and bugs—and private, too. In addition, decks can feature structures such as screened rooms, gazebos, pergolas, and trellises. They can even help you save money on cooling bills if built to shade a lower level. Best of all, an upgraded deck does not need to cost a lot more than a bare-bones one. The design ideas and advice you'll find on the following pages of *1001 Ideas for Decks* will help you get the most from the deck addition you're planning for your home.

An Easier Approach to Deck Design

To design anything, you must gather all the bits and pieces you'd like to include and then try to put them together in a coherent and elegant way. Decks are no exception. You'll want to know where the sun passes over your property in the summer, which views of your yard you prefer, which architectural elements to borrow to help the deck blend with your home—and much more.

One way to gather the pieces is the scrapbook approach. Clip photos of decks you like from home design magazines, and then hand them over to a designer or builder and say, "I

Below Though it contains many traditional features (pool, spa, planters, etc.), this deck is designed to stand out with its fresh color scheme and contemporary styling.

want something like this." However, it is well worth the effort to go one step further and look at all the options an architect would. By taking the time to consider all the angles, you will end up with a deck that perfectly suits your home and lifestyle.

Successful deck design is about seeing all of the possibilities. We've identified those that are the most important and devoted a chapter to each of them. Part 1 focuses on fundamental deck design principles. It will help you envision key aspects of your deck, such as where to put it, how big to make it, and what height

Right This deck designer used the same colors, shingles, and trim on the deck as found on the house to create a unified, seamless look.

Below right Outfitting your deck with comfortable furniture, a stone fireplace, and columns can make it feel more like a cozy den than a traditional deck.

and shape it should be. It also addresses key concerns, such as material selection and safety.

Part 2 is about getting more from your deck. It suggests ways to make it more comfortable, more practical, and, in a word, more fun. Still need a little help to get your creative juices flowing? Part 3 of *1001 Ideas for Decks* is a gallery of successful decks that combine many fundamental deck design principles and then some. Many examples were created by top architects and designers.

After looking at the photos and drawings in Parts 1, 2, and 3, you'll have a clearer understanding of the deck design process and its possibilities, whether you go on to design your own deck or turn your notes and sketches over to a professional. Or you can turn to page 244 to see professionally designed deck plans you can purchase.

Part 1

Deck Design Basics

Chapter 1

Where to Put It

Choosing the right site for your deck may seem obvious; nevertheless, it's worth thinking through all of the possibilities. You're bound to discover surprises, some pleasant and others not. For example, where are the best views? Hop on a ladder, climb to deck height, and check them out. While you're there, anticipate the views of your deck from neighbors' windows and yards. Will you be able to create the privacy you need with privacy screens or overhead structures? What is the best way to build around items that would be difficult and expensive to move, such as natural rock outcroppings, trees, and basement doors?

The location of most decks will often be determined by the interior room (or rooms) you want to connect it to. For a deck used to cook and serve meals, connecting to the kitchen or dining room is imperative. For sunbathing and spa splashing, locate your deck off a family room, basement room, or spare bedroom. There are plenty of possibilities for locating elevated decks as well, including bedrooms, bathrooms, over-the-garage recreation rooms, and hallways.

Other site considerations include the style of your home's exterior. The best location for a deck may be trumped because it will destroy a key feature of your home. Or, the best site may be too expensive to build on because of uneven or unstable terrain. Exposure to sun and wind are also important considerations, although they can be mitigated by careful planning. Finally, call all utilities to learn the locations of buried water, gas, sewer, and electric lines.

This understated ground-level deck provides easy access to the yard and keeps arresting water views intact.

The Importance of Exposure

Assuming you have more than one option for where to build your deck, exposure to the sun may be the deciding factor. Sun exposure is determined by the proposed deck's orientation to the sun's daily path. A south-facing deck will receive sun almost all day. East- and west-facing decks get sun in the morning and afternoon, respectively. Southeast- or southwest-facing decks will receive the sun for longer periods than decks that face due east or west. North-facing decks, unless extended beyond the shadow of your house, will receive little or no sun for much of the day.

To decide what's best for you, think about when you'll be using your deck. If it's for your morning coffee, southeast- or east-facing may be your preference. An afternoon and evening user would probably prefer a southwest- or west-facing deck. If you live in a climate where summers are cool, perhaps south-facing is the ideal orientation. Conversely, if you live where it's warm most of the time, a northern exposure may suit you.

Of course, you will need to take into account the shade thrown by nearby trees and buildings. Keep in mind that you can always create shade by planting trees or adding an overhead shade structure, such as a pergola or gazebo. Also note that you can wrap your deck around two sides of your house to take advantage of both sun and shade.

In many locations, wind is another factor to consider. If you live in a cool climate where the prevailing wind is frequently gusty, opt for the protected side of your house to increase the time you can spend on your deck. If that's not possible, you can build a wind screen. (See page 144.) If you live in a hot climate, the breeze may bring welcome relief from the heat.

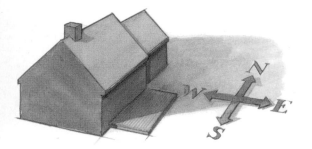

East-Facing Deck

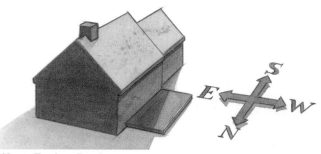

West-Facing Deck

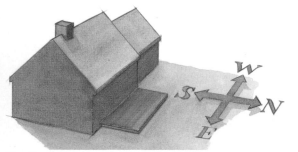

North-Facing Deck

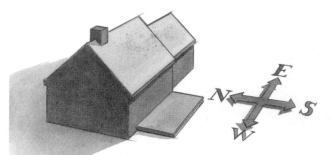

South-Facing Deck

Above This southwest-facing deck is mostly sunny from the afternoon through the evening in the summer.

Fit the Deck to Your Floor Plan

In addition to creating outdoor living space for you, your family, and your guests, a good deck design can improve your home's floor plan. For example, a deck can extend the area of a small room, such as a bedroom or dining room. It can also connect two areas of the home, improving traffic flow from one part of the house to another. Decks are often used to join a kitchen and family room. Multilevel decks can connect an upper level of your home to a lower level or to the yard. Wraparound decks can connect two parts of both your house and yard, which is especially useful when the terrain around your home is rough. Your design can also allow for an entirely new room, such as an outdoor entertainment area or a secluded retreat.

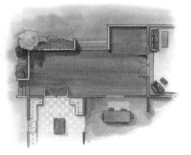

Connecting Kitchen to Living Room

Connecting Second Story to Yard

Connecting Front to Back

1 This redwood deck connects the family room and living room, creating one large space for entertaining. Pillars, topped by lights, provide privacy from the left.

2 The raised wraparound deck here provides a direct path to several rooms of the house, including the screened porch, while offering many places to enjoy the terraced gardens.

1

2

Smart Tip **Locate Hidden Obstacles**

Check out the location of everything on your property that is near the planned construction site. Chances are, the deck will limit access to, or interfere with, at least one of them. It's common, for example, to have exterior spigots end up below deck level. You can either relocate them or build a small trap door for access. Also, do not plan to build near a septic tank. Setbacks of 15 to 20 feet are usually required. Other in-ground obstacles may include buried water piping, electrical lines to the garage or pool, gas lines to the barbecue, sump pump and rainwater drains, basement doors, and buried oil tanks.

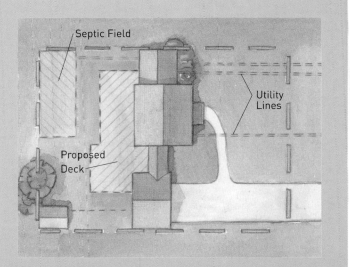

Under the yard there is more going on than most of us think. Be sure to check before you dig.

Design Tip **Consider the Unusual**

While there are many more possibilities open to you when designing a new home, you may be surprised at what you can do when adding on—especially when your deck addition is part of a bigger remodeling project. Think outside the box. An entry deck, with the addition of trellises for privacy, may provide the traditional front-porch feel you've always wanted. Adding a master suite above the garage? Build a balcony to the front or back, or wrap it around three sides. A pocket deck off a first-level bathroom, enveloped with greenery, might just become a perfect retreat for when you need to take a break from the mad rush of daily life. Equip it with an outdoor shower, and you'll come to know what luxury really means.

❶

❷

1 A western red cedar balcony deck located over the front door does double duty: it provides a place to watch the world go by and offers shelter from bad weather at the front door.

2 Extending a deck over the garage door will make your garage feel bigger, especially in rainy weather. And it won't block daylight from your primary living space.

3 This deck was notched into the roof. It affords great views and private lounging. A floor drain carries away rain and melt-off from snow and ice.

The Right Height

In many situations, though not all, you will have some flexibility as to how high you build your deck. A first-level deck, for example, can go anywhere from a few inches above ground level to a few inches below the level of the interior floor. The height of a second-level deck may be more limited. There are existing windows above and below as well as door placement to consider. No matter where you're planning to put your deck, the general guideline is to build it as low as you can. Doing so will make it less complex to build, safer to use, less costly, less likely to interfere with views from windows and patio doors, easier to make private, and more likely to blend with the house and yard. It will also take up less of your yard with space-consuming stairs. If you do want an upper-story deck, make it as small as you can while still meeting your needs. Doing so will make it easier to fit with the style of your home and won't put the lower floor in perpetual shadow.

1 This small wraparound deck is 4 in. below door thresholds, helping to avoid infiltration of snow and rain.

2 The same deck is also only two easy steps off the grade, eliminating the need for railings and allowing access from anywhere.

3 With new home construction, such as this lighthouse-inspired design, the deck can be planned at the same time as the rest of the house, allowing for more height options.

3

Smart Tip **Cut Cooling Bills**

A south-facing elevated deck (on a second or third level) can be an energy-saver. In the summer, with the sun at a high trajectory, the deck will shade windows and doors and keep the lower level cool. In the winter, when the sun crosses the southern sky at a lower angle, south-facing windows and patio doors on the level below the deck will receive the sun and its warmth. Such a deck should not be built too deep—about 6 feet in most locations works well.

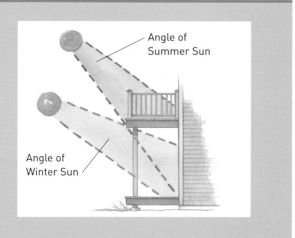

Angle of Summer Sun

Angle of Winter Sun

1

1 A second-story deck, if not too wide, will allow solar heat gain through first-level windows and doors in the winter and provide shade in the summer.

2 A low, ground-level deck is the easiest to mesh with house architecture and landscape.

1

2

1 This mahogany deck add-on was dropped several steps below the bedroom patio doors to preserve the view.

2 With the guardrail out of the way, there's a view even from the bed.

3 A custom guardrail, made with stainless-steel rods, is nearly invisible. A stainless-steel rail support helped to keep the number of posts to a minimum as well.

3

Maximize Your Best Views

Where you place your deck will largely determine your view. Off a second or third floor, it will be expansive. Nearer to the ground, you'll have a better vantage of your yard and garden, but not much else. Unless you have something special to look at though, opt for the latter for the reasons already mentioned (cost, ease of construction, safety, privacy, etc.). If you do have a great view, make the most of it and locate your deck accordingly. If your view is mixed, block out the eyesore with a well-placed fence (built on the deck) or trellis. Trees, hedges, and shrubs can also detract or hide what you'd rather not look at.

1 Take your deck to the view with a patio deck, such as this stream-side hideaway.

2 With a solid guardrail you can have your view and privacy, too.

3 A rectangular bumpout, such as this one, offers an unobstructed, 180-deg. view.

1 If the deck is open to public view, as is this western red cedar balcony deck, use screening to ensure privacy.

2 Consider putting a spa on the lowest level of the deck, where it will be easiest to create a sense of privacy.

3 This deck and pool, surrounded by the house on three sides and a natural stone outcropping on the other, are completely private.

Ensure Privacy

Deck placement will also affect your privacy. Once again, keep your deck's height low if you can. It will eliminate most privacy problems or make them a lot easier to solve. If you do find that your preferred deck location is in view of your neighbors, trellises, deck-top fences, and plantings can help. A solid guardrail, especially for a raised deck, can also create the privacy you require. When creating privacy with a fence or plantings, take care not to inadvertently block a view your neighbor values (of a lake, for instance). If you have no choice, install a privacy screen that can be removed or rolled up when your deck is not in use. (See page 156.) Outdoor curtains, made with a weather-resistant fabric, are also a gracious solution.

Use Natural Assets

Rough, steep, or uneven terrain in a backyard is normally a liability. When designing a deck, however, you may be able to turn it to your advantage. A moderately sloping site may be a natural for a multilevel deck that steps down (or up) the incline. With a steep slope, a deck may be your only way to have a bit of backyard—and the view is likely to be interesting. Large rock outcroppings or boulders provide natural focal points for your deck project and should also be considered an asset that is worked into the design. Trees are often allowed to penetrate decks, but this can be a tricky detail. (See page 200.)

1 The large tree and stone outcroppings on the site of this deck were left undisturbed by the architect. The tree penetrates the deck through a tightly scribed opening, while the stone is left unskirted and open to view.

2 This deck also accommodates mature trees with its interesting zigzag shape.

3 A large stone outcropping turned into a rock garden helps merge this composite deck with its tropical setting.

Tools of the Trade

Good scale drawings of your home's floor plan (the level from which you plan to access the deck) and of the surrounding yard are essential for beginning the design process. Together, they are the best way to see the relationships between existing interior rooms and possible deck locations. You'll probably need to draw it yourself on a large piece of paper, but site plans, property surveys, and building plans will all help. Make copies and draw in possible deck locations. Whenever possible, create deck boundaries by continuing previously existing lines or by echoing existing shapes.

To help determine the elevations of your deck, photograph the possible deck locations with a digital camera. Download the images to your computer, make several printouts, and sketch in possible elevations. When you have the ones you like, transfer them to graph paper. You can also use deck and landscape design software, but unless you're familiar with it, there is a steep learning curve involved. Digital cameras allow you to try out many ideas quickly and inexpensively.

1 Take digital photos of your chosen deck locations, and make printouts of each. Then sketch in possible deck scenarios.

2 The finished projects starts with a drawing on graph paper (opposite, top right). You'll need them to get your building permit. They're also helpful if you seek professional design help.

1

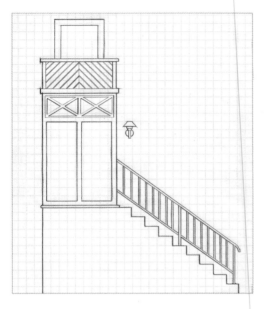

Smart Tip **Rule Review**

It's wise to become familiar with building codes, as well as restrictions set by homeowner associations, historical commissions, and zoning departments, before you begin to design your deck. Some of the key things you will need to know include allowable setbacks (minimum distance of deck from property lines), guardrail and stair-rail height requirements, baluster spacing requirements, and restrictions about being able to see your deck from the street in a historical district. Some homeowner associations may even specify architectural styles and finish colors.

Chapter 2

Determine Size and Shape

Decks are a relatively inexpensive way to add square feet to a home, so many homeowners tend to build decks that are bigger than they actually need, feeling that they'll find a way to use the space. But big is not always better.

Aside from the obvious drawback of adding to the cost of the project, a bigger deck will require more maintenance, gobble up prime space for gardening and other activities, and make it harder to achieve a look that fits the style of your house. A large deck, for example, will make an average-size house look smaller; a small house is liable to be overwhelmed.

Whether your deck will comprise one activity area or several, plan carefully so that you build only what you need. Make a list of all the ways you plan to use the deck, and determine approximately how much space you'll need for each of them. Use your deck plan to map out likely locations for your activities. For a deck to accommodate an eating area for six, a

lounging area (that can double as a secondary eating area during larger gatherings), and a cooking area, you will need between 150 and 200 square feet.

Avoid built-ins that force you to use space in only one way—unless you're sure you're going to be using them a lot. For example, a permanent fire pit surrounded by built-in benches may seem like a wonderful idea, but unless you intend to use it more than a dozen times a year, you may want to consider using a portable fireplace and the chairs from your patio set instead.

This deck is divided into separate activity areas. Its design provides adequate room for dining, grilling, and lounging.

1 One-room decks are generally single purpose, such as this dining deck that's directly off the kitchen. There is, however, plenty of room for a grill, should the homeowners choose to use one.

2 Move the lounge chairs aside, and this "one-room" deck is ready to stage a dinner party.

One-Room Decks

It's often helpful to think of the various activity areas of a deck or yard as "rooms." Decks, therefore, can have one or more rooms. Versatility is the operative word if you're planning a one-room deck. If the space is small, opt for small-scale, lightweight furniture that doesn't take up a lot of room and can be easily moved, folded, or stacked; a grill that can be moved easily in order to free up space for other activities; and wide stair treads that can double as seating. Multipurpose furniture, such as a bench that doubles as a table and has storage below, is worth considering. Hammocks can quickly turn a small deck into a napping place, but integrate the support posts into your design so that you won't have to deal with a hammock stand.

If you need a large deck, plan on using planters, screens, and trellises to create cozy areas as you need them. Otherwise, big decks can feel unwelcoming when you want an outdoor breakfast for two. Canopies and gazebos can create a sense of enclosure as well.

1

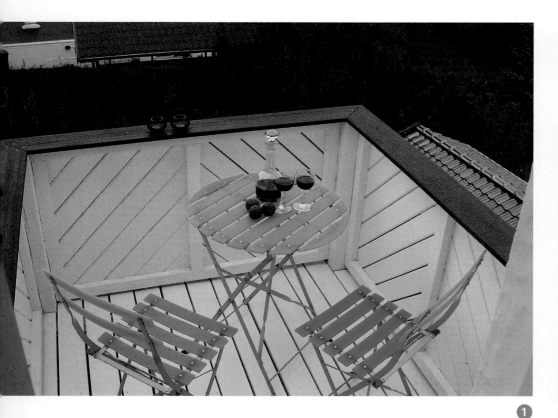

1 A balcony deck, built over a side entrance, provides a quiet retreat for a busy home. (See pages 34–35 for additional photos.)

2 The space below the balcony was enclosed to create an energy-saving airtight entry.

3 Conceived as an outdoor living room, this versatile one-room deck is complete with outdoor carpeting and plush furniture.

Multiple-Room Decks

You might feel that some deck activities are mutually exclusive and need their own dedicated space. In such cases, you may want two or more "rooms" for your deck. You may not want to be beside the grill or dining table, for example, while you're trying to sunbathe or use the spa. Similarly, an on-deck play area for children might be better separate from adult entertainment areas. Sometimes homeowners choose multiroom decks for needs other than space. For example, you may want to capture a view or take advantage of a sunny exposure with your second deck room. Such decks often wrap around one or two corners of a house. Multiple rooms can be separated by changes in level, jogs in the footprint of your house, planters, trellises, privacy screens, and even drapes.

1 This spa alcove is private without feeling completely shut off from the rest of the deck, so bathers won't feel isolated.

2 The "rooms" of this deck are defined by the use of railings, changes in level, balustrades, and walls.

❶

❷

1 This three-level deck gradually descends to the yard while creating separate areas for grilling, lounging, and dining.

2 In addition to level changes, running the redwood deck boards at differing angles sets "rooms" apart from each other.

3 A large deck with many "rooms" is ideal for large gatherings that mix kids and adults. It also reduces mowing chores!

Choose a Shape

The design of your house and backyard are often the deciding factors when it comes to selecting a deck shape. In fact, it's a good idea to start the process by deciding whether your deck is a "house deck" or a "yard deck." In the first case, the deck is closer and more connected to the house, typically raised 4 feet or more. A yard deck is more connected to the landscape. It's generally close to the ground and may incorporate planting beds and other natural features, such as trees and rocks. In general, house decks will look better if they echo the shape of the house, which in most cases is rectangular or square. Yard-oriented decks can take on more irregular or organic shapes. Curves and polygons tend to lend themselves to decks that are transitional, or somewhere in between house- and yard-oriented. Such shapes may also be useful when connecting a series of deck "rooms."

1 Running a deck parallel with the lines of the house is an easy way to determine your deck shape, but there are variations you can make to add interest, as you'll see in the following chapters.

2 Another approach is to extend the existing lines of the house. In this architect-designed home, the deck width is the same as the room it extends. In addition, the shape matches those of the roof and patio below for a unified look.

3 Square or almost-square decks accommodate a wider variety of activities than long, narrow, rectangular decks.

1 When a house does have some curves to it, like the arched roof and bowed face of this house, corresponding shapes in the decking and railings work especially well. Composites make the bending easier.

2 The wide curve of this raised deck echoes the arched transom over the patio doors and seems well suited to a home built of large, round western red cedar logs.

Design Tip **Go Slow on Curves**

There's no question about it; curves are sexy. When it comes to decks, however, use caution. Curves are often expensive to produce and rarely relate to the architecture of a house. Bowed shapes off one side of a square or rectangular deck—especially when half-round windows are present—are an exception. Gentle curves also fit right in when there are natural curves in the landscape, such as round tree crowns, glacial boulders, or the edge of a pond. Curved deck shapes can also help integrate a ground-level deck with a hilly terrain.

Gentle curves, as displayed by this redwood deck, are easier to integrate with house and yard than U-shapes with tight radii.

2

Smart Tip **Allow Enough Space**

Don't make your deck too small. Consider all possible activities, and use the following guidelines to ensure adequate space.

Eating areas: The area of the table plus 4 to 5 feet of clearance in all directions for easy circulation.

Grilling areas: The area of the grill and food preparation counter (often built into the grill); 2 feet of clearance to the guardrail, wood structures, and house siding; 4 to 5 feet of clearance for areas subject to traffic.

Lounging or sitting areas: The area for each chair or lounge plus about 2 feet of clearance in front of and between chairs. Keep seating well away from any deck edge that has no guardrail, such as near stairs.

Traffic paths: 4 to 5 feet wide.

Spas and hot tubs: The area of the spa and a 4- to 5-foot clearance between the spa and adjacent areas subject to activity or traffic. Ideally, allow for access from at least two directions, and incorporate an ample lounging area for sunning.

Fire pits: The area of the fire-pit cutout in addition to manufacturer-recommended clearances between it and nearby structures, such as guardrails, trellises, and overhead shade structures. (One typical gas-fired fire pit recommends a 3-foot side clearance and 7-foot ceiling clearance.) Locate fire pits so that prevailing winds do not cause smoke to become a nuisance.

1 As with curved decks, polygonal-shaped decks usually work best when they mimic the contours of the house.

2 On this traditional-style house, the covered western red cedar deck plays off the windowed lookout above it.

3 The decking continues the octagonal theme, with long planks connecting pillars to the center point.

4 This two-story polygonal deck complements the hip roof above it and adds interest and balance to an otherwise ordinary facade.

❹

Chapter 3

Getting On and Off

Most decks will benefit by having at least two ways to get access to them from the yard and two from the house. One yard entrance, for instance, can permit a short walk to the back door of the garage, while the other leads to gardens or the pool. Access to small, second-story decks is the exception to the rule. One yard entrance is usually all that is feasible.

On decks less than 3 feet high, wide yard-to-deck entrances are more gracious and can open up a view that would otherwise be obstructed by guardrails. They also allow the stair treads to be used as bleachers for watching backyard volleyball without restricting traffic. Wide entrances may not be feasible for decks more than 3 feet high because the stairs take up too much yard space.

On decks less than 2 feet off the ground, you may eliminate guardrails altogether and allow access from anywhere. Be cautious about doing so, however, especially if the deck is small. It's too easy to step backward, off the edge. Furniture placement be- comes more challenging, too—you may need to put your dining table in the middle of the deck so a diner can't back a chair off the edge.

Patio doors are the most practical house-to-deck transitions. They afford you a view of your deck and yard and come in a variety of configurations. Choose the widest door that will fit to your plan. French-style doors make roomy, graceful transitions. Adding a second door from house to deck will take the pressure off a heavily-trafficked back door.

Folding walls offer the most dramatic of all house-to-deck transitions. The deck and adjoining room literally become one space.

Door Options

There are two main categories of patio doors from which to choose: sliders (also called gliders) and hinged. Sliders save space because there is no need to accommodate door swing. If you go for a slider, invest in a quality unit with a secure locking system. A sticking door quickly becomes tiresome, so look for heavy-duty sills and stainless-steel or nylon ball-bearing rollers. Consider a unit with a sliding screen that automatically closes behind you so that you're not constantly asking kids to close the screen door. Today's sliding patio doors are available with wide stiles and rails that mimic the look of French doors. Extra-wide, three- and four-panel sliders are great for opening up your view.

There are several types of hinged patio doors. The simplest is a single, one-panel glass door. You can also order a two-panel hinged door with one or two operating panels. With one operating panel, you will have to decide which panel you want fixed. Triple-panel doors are also available.

Doors can be ordered as either in- or out-swinging. In addition, they can be hinged on the right or left side. You have lots of options, so think them through carefully with a catalog in hand to avoid mistakes. Avoid choosing a door configuration that will interfere with traffic or furniture, such as an out-swing door that blocks access to deck stairs or an in-swing door that cramps the seating for your kitchen table.

Screen doors complicate matters further. Double patio doors with a single out-swing door, for example, may give you more space inside but are often paired with an indoor sliding screen. You may not want the screen frame blocking the wood frame of your new, expensive patio door. An in-swing version of the same door typically comes with a sliding screen on the outside. Double patio doors with two in-swinging doors, however, will require double out-swinging screen doors or a single out-swing screen door and one fixed screen panel.

1 These side-by-side sliders offer multiple ways onto the deck, which is key for one that runs the length of the house.

2 A four-panel sliding door with no middle barrier is great for bringing out large platters and trays without having to turn sideways.

1 This large arched transom draws attention to the high ceilings while opening up the view to the deck.

2 A small room may only allow for a patio door with one operable panel, but stationary panels give the illusion of a grander entrance.

3 The out-swinging double French doors clear the way for the waterfront views from this master bedroom.

2

Smart Tip **Designing Your Doors**

Door design trends continue to move toward more glass. Sidelights, stationary panels, and transoms combine to offer panoramic views. With that much exposure, energy efficiency is vital. Look for Energy Star qualified products, and check for product ratings with the National Fenestration Rating Council (NFRC) at www.nfrc.org. Buying energy-efficient doors may entitle you to tax benefits. You can also check with your building products supplier for the glazing most appropriate for your climate and exposure. Lower your maintenance with doors that are clad with aluminum on the exterior. For looks, you have many grille options and even decorative glass panels, but views of your new deck will probably be the best decoration.

3

Folding Walls

If you're longing to bring serious drama to your deck, consider blurring the line between indoors and out-doors with a folding-wall system. These doors go be-yond multiple-panel doors by running the entire length of the wall, with no obstruction to the outside when opened. New products have evolved from their European predecessors to fit the needs of homes on this side of the Atlantic. These dramatic openings are dynamic yet practical, making the outdoor space part and parcel of your kitchen, dining area, or even your bedroom.

There are several types of folding walls, including aluminum, wood with exterior aluminum cladding, and all wood. There is even an all-glass option with no rails or stiles. Mechanically speaking, door panels slide along a top-hung or floor-mounted track and stack separately or fold at hinges for stowage. If you live in an area subject to hurricanes, check to be sure your folding-wall manufacturer has a Dade County hurricane-approved system. Keep insects out using a roll-down screen or one that is pleated and slides.

Installing a folding wall system is not a weekend do-it-yourself project. Use professional help to ensure that the opening does not sag over time and impede opening or closing the system.

Right The curved stack-away wall system that opens this living room to a deck has a storage bay where the panels slide when opened.

Folding-Type Open Wall

The main consideration for choosing your folding wall is deciding how the doors should fold. Depending on the manufacturer and model, the doors can be inward or outward folding and can accommodate certain angles in the door design. In the long run, you may be better off with a top-hung system versus a floor-mounted one because the top track supports most of the weight and is less subject to dirt and debris than bottom-track systems.

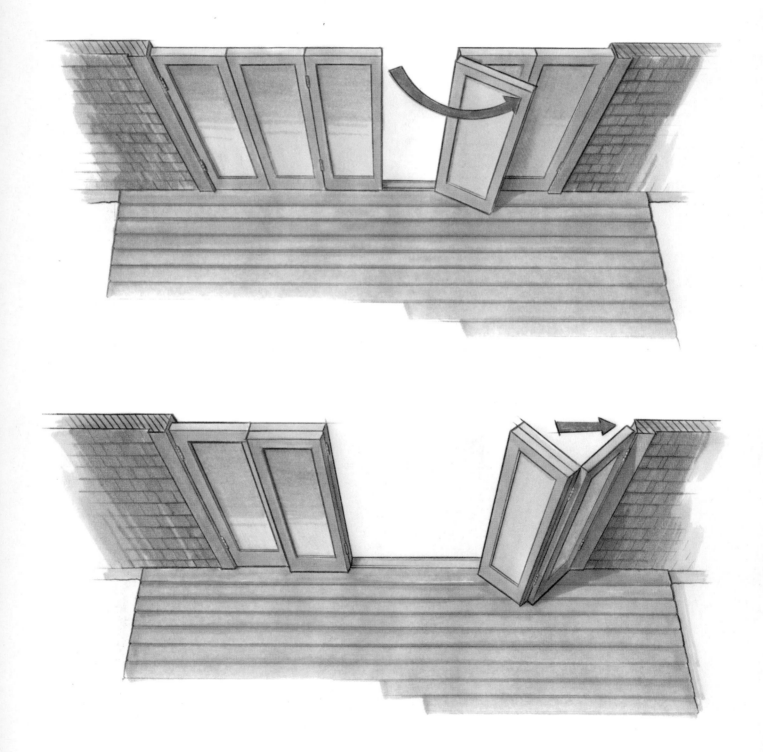

Stacking-Type Open Wall

The advantage with this system is that door panels store completely out of sight into a storage bay (though you will need to make room for this indoors). Slide-and-stack door panels can also handle curves, unlike their folding-wall cousin. Here the choice is made between horizontal or vertical rollers. Horizontal rollers can traverse 90-degree angles, which translates into more stacking options. Units with vertical rollers, however, can be stacked closer together in tighter spaces.

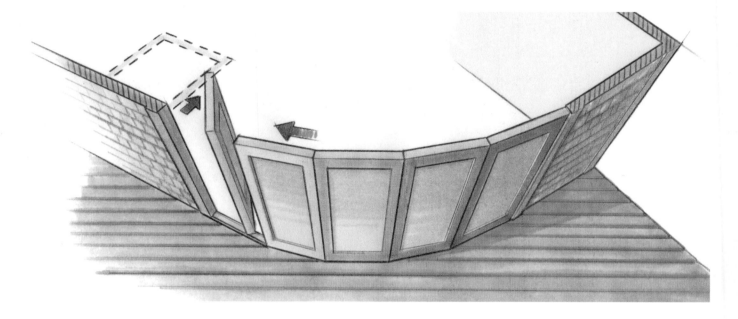

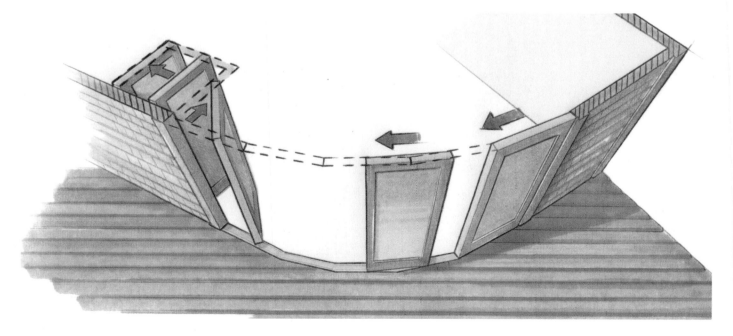

Stair Design

Just about any raised deck requires stairs—at least if you want to get to the yard from the deck. For a ground-level deck, it may be a simple step or two. You may even get away with not needing a handrail in some locales, depending on building codes. For decks that are more than 3 or 4 feet above grade, stairs become more complex—so much so that they're often left until the end of the construction project when it's easier to visualize how to construct them. Don't wait until then, however, to design them. Poorly planned stairs can be an eyesore.

If you've kept the height of your deck low or made it a multilevel deck that steps down to ground level gradually, your job will be a lot easier. High decks require stairs with lots of steps that consume space and require significant additional labor. Stairs with turns and landings are generally less obtrusive and less daunting to climb than those without. Stairs that follow natural grade contours, where possible, are also less obtrusive. Spiral stairs take up the least amount of space but are not so easy to negotiate.

1 Wide treads with low risers make for a more comfortable climb.

2 These western red cedar stairs connect the screened porch with the upper and lower decks and the pool—without looking ungainly or obtrusive.

❶

Design Tip **Lessen Visibility of Stairs**

Most designers recommend stairs with a minimum 3-foot width and that you treat the handrail the same as you've treated the guardrail. With long stairs, this may create too much visual clutter, so you may want to use a less visible metal handrail system. Painted black or white, depending on the background, such handrails almost disappear from a distance.

3

1 Stairs that abut an exterior wall, such as these, will be less obtrusive than those that reach into the yard.

2 For a period-style house with bold detailing, you may want the railings to stand out, as they do here.

3 Cable rail systems give stair handrails a lighter, more contemporary look.

4 The stairs to this Victorian-influenced deck are discreetly tucked away to either side, keeping the rear elevation of the house visually unencumbered.

2

4

2

3

4

1 Spiral stairs are a compact way to connect a second-story deck with the yard.

2 Fill the space where stairs turn with planters, and use benches in place of guardrails where allowed by code.

3 A handrail without cable or balusters is permissible against a wall but not along a stairs' open side.

4 A stairs' handrail is subject to many of the same code restrictions as a deck guardrail, including a maximum 4-in. opening between balusters.

On-Deck Traffic

Be generous when sizing the main traffic "corridors" of your deck by allowing at least 4 feet so that the traffic lanes can accommodate two people walking abreast. Allow at least 4 feet around activity areas where people will circulate, such as a dining or conversation area. Locate potentially hazardous activity areas away from traffic corridors. For example, put the cooking area where people will not have to pass close by to get somewhere else. Ditto for tripping hazards, such as steps, and cutouts for ponds, spas, trees, or through-deck gardens. If your deck is small, use items such as benches, planters, and trellises to define traffic paths. A small counter, for example, may be all you need to force kids to walk around a

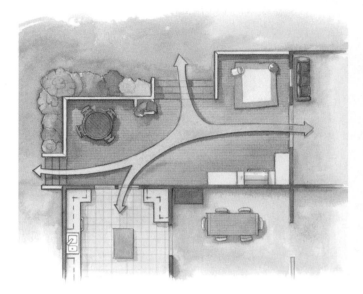

grilling area rather than through it. A bench that's built around a through-deck planter will prevent visitors from stepping off the edge.

❶

1 The grilling area on this deck is conveniently located near both the kitchen and the outdoor dining area—but is railed off from, and out of the way of, traffic.

2 Traffic is facilitated on this deck with a wide corridor in front of the screened porch, as well as two side doors for the porch itself.

3 Bump out your deck to create a spacious dining area that has plenty of clearance between railings and chairs and is out of the flow of traffic.

Improve Yard Traffic

Decks can improve how you navigate your yard by serving as both deck and path. A deck that wraps around the corner of a house may be used to connect a back door and a garage, or even a front and back door. Deck paths can lead guests to an attractive view or garden bed. They're also great for joining the house with outbuildings, such as detached garages, gazebos, pool houses, and greenhouses.

1 The breezeway between the house and the garage isn't just for shelter; it doubles as a porch.

2 This deck walkway connects the house and garden with the garden shed.

3 Wide platform stair treads are a graceful way to handle access from deck to yard across a sloping terrain.

Chapter 4

What's Your Style?

The traditional advice about choosing a deck style is to make it conform to the architectural style of your house. Look to basic shapes, details, materials, and colors, say most designers, to determine which design direction to head in. It's good advice, especially if your home has a distinctive period style. A classic California deck, for example, would be ill suited to a New England farmhouse.

The reality of many of today's homes, however, is that they are a mélange of styles—or else they have no discernible style at all. If your house is "traditional" with elements from various architectural styles or if it has few architectural details at all, which is the case with many post-war split-levels and ranches, your deck style choices are broader. You can keep it simple or choose a complementary style. For example, add a dash of rustic to a 1950s ranch with a deck made of rough-sawn timbers. Or choose a Japanese theme with a gated entrance, a bridge, and appropriately arranged stones. Yes, you'd be venturing away from conventional wisdom—but top designers are the first to do the same, so you're in good company.

Don't hesitate to seek design help. A well-designed deck will add interest and value to a house with a boring facade. Deck styling also allows you to get personal: love wind chimes? Create a symphony. The ocean? Start beachcombing for buoys and driftwood. Tropical islands? Think thatch and brightly colored shade cloth. Your deck is a blank canvas.

Decks can be adapted to a wide variety of styles. The Adirondack styling of this deck's custom guardrail suits the bucolic setting.

The History of Decks

The traditional deck—a wood platform with guardrails, stairs, and perhaps a shade structure—is a relatively new architectural innovation. It first became popular in the 1950s and 60s, partly because the quickly-built housing that went up after World War II did not have proper porches. As "the greatest generation" began filling the millions of small split-levels, ranches, and raised ranches with baby boomers, decks were a low-cost, easy way to expand living space. Unfortunately, not a lot of design savvy went into many of those early decks. To make matters worse, the deck-building craze spread to older homes as well—but again without much common design sense.

In recent decades, deck design has begun to mature, but many development homes are still erected with decks that look like they're from a Nixon-era plan book. It's no wonder that many homeowners in recent years have shunned decks in favor of stone patios and terraces. News about the hazards of CCA (chromated copper arsenate) pressure-treated wood and the considerable maintenance that some wood decks require has not improved their image.

Decks, however, do have their place. In addition to being easier and less costly to build, more practical, and more comfortable to use than equivalent masonry solutions, decks are in a better position to keep up with changing needs. As we react to the excesses of outlandishly large manses and our SUV culture rediscovers simplicity and economy, it's likely that homeowners and designers will take a new look at decks—and the design pendulum will swing again.

1 Decks are the new porch, having evolved from traditional structures, such as the one shown here.

2 Today, decks that work the best are often designed at the same time as the house, allowing them to be completely integrated. Here, a western red cedar deck wraps the entire second story.

3 Add-on decks, however, can enhance almost any home. This redwood deck provides an entryway as welcoming as any porch.

Today's Decks

Compare many of today's custom decks with those of a decade or two ago and you're likely to find that they blend better with house and landscape. Improved railing systems, composite decking and trim materials, and a greater range of color are all contributing factors. There are, however, other influences. A resurgence of interest in gardening has bedecked even modest decks in blossoms and greenery from spring to fall. A greater consciousness about the importance of good design has made decks lighter feeling and less obtrusive than the heavy, overbuilt structures of the past. The same style changes that have affected indoor design and decoration have migrated outside—allowing deck design to become more eclectic, minimal, romantic, whimsical, or rustic.

1 This composite deck takes a cue from Asia, incorporating a yin-yang theme with a soothing koi pond and rock gardens.

2 These homeowners found the right niche in their house plan for this deck; then they borrowed the siding and trim colors to create a unified look.

❶

1 An eclectic design approach takes the best from all worlds. Here, contemporary furnishings mix with red railings, white siding, and splashes of bright, beautiful geraniums.

2 These homeowners pay homage to a seaside setting with all-natural wood tones, teak furniture, and found objects.

1

Smart Tip **Deck Design Software**

Software programs are available to homeowners who want to create their own deck and landscape plans. They simplify designing decks, railings, planters, and other deck amenities and allow you to view everything in three dimensions. All software comes with tutorials, although there is a steep learning curve to using these programs. Basic architectural knowledge is helpful. Certain programs are more user-friendly than others, offering drop-and-drag existing designs that can be modified to suit your needs. Others offer the ability to import digital photos of your home as a starting point for the design process. Helpful features to look for when buying software include virtual tours (the ability to see your yard or deck from any vantage point), cost estimators, programs that can produce detailed materials lists, and plant encyclopedias. Some software packages have a feature that won't allow you to produce a plan that doesn't conform to the national building code.

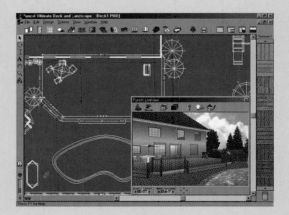

Period Pieces

Designing a deck for an older home can be a real challenge. While decks often look natural on homes built after World War II, such as ranches and split-levels, they are often an awkward fit for Victorian, Tudor, and Spanish-style homes. Even early Colonials, Colonial revivals of the 1920s and 30s, and capes can be overpowered visually by a deck if it's not carefully designed. In such cases, architects often keep decks unobtrusive and low to the ground, often eliminating the need for railings. Another approach is to choose a porch-like design for your deck. New tongue-and-groove synthetic decking looks like the narrow wood planks often used for porch floors, but it can withstand the elements with little maintenance. It's particularly important with period homes to keep the deck in the scale of the house. Some designers suggest that the deck shouldn't be bigger than the biggest room in the house.

Finally, work hard to integrate architectural elements from the house into the deck. Borrow from the profiles of existing columns when choosing balusters; pick up fluting details from columns, and use them on deck posts; mimic the width of fascias and pilasters. Look to your home's water table (boards installed below siding on some older homes) for ideas on how to trim out the perimeter of your deck.

1 Sometimes the only solution for an older home is not a deck but a porch, especially when it will be visible from the street.

2 Decks can also combine aspects of both deck and porch, as shown here.

1

2

1 This column-perched deck, part of an addition to a nineteenth-century school house, serves the master bedroom.

2 It is echoed by a pergola attached to the garage, creating a sort of bookends for the yard.

3 Color and a higher degree of finish help decks feel at home with antique houses, such as this Tudor. In addition, the arbor "roof" has the same pitch as the dormer above.

3

4

4 Closed skirting panels, except for vents, give this deck a visual solidity that's in keeping with this period.

5 A hot tub in matching redwood is discretely tucked away next to a privacy wall and does not look out of place with this older home.

6 Other details that help carry the theme: the handrail, post caps, and decorative balusters.

5

6

Custom Guardrails

If your home is architecturally distinctive, consider installing a custom guardrail that echoes an existing architectural element, such as flared siding or existing fretwork. Even if your house's architecture is not unusual, you may want to consider a custom guardrail. For example, ranches usually have a horizontal look that merges well with gardens and landscaping. To retain this quality, you may choose a solid guardrail or one with an open grid rather than using the traditional vertical balusters. Wrought steel balustrades with serpentine, curved, or concentric designs might be just the touch to dress up a raised ranch. Keep in mind that custom work will add to the job's cost. Working with a local fabricator or mill to cut or bend repetitive components may be cheaper (and better) than cutting them on site.

1 Steel piping, combined with wood, is an effective way to create simple yet sophisticated-looking guardrails.

2 Intricate designs in metalwork add a bit of the unexpected to a deck while casting interesting shadows.

3 Stainless-steel cables are best for keeping views intact. Use with a custom wood guardrail design, as shown here, or with metal posts designed for cable.

3

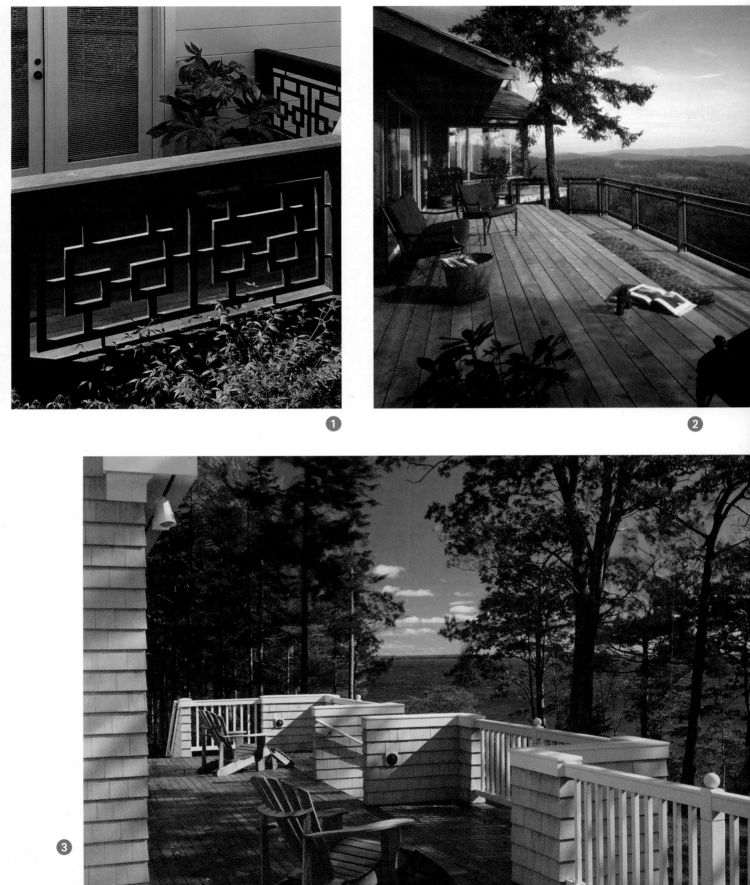

1 This Oriental-style balustrade was crafted with redwood for lasting beauty.

2 Glass guardrails can be fabricated with wood posts and rails, as shown, or assembled from prefabricated components.

3 Take a chance and experiment when designing guardrails; alternating solid and open railings ties the deck to the house without blocking out all the light and scenery.

4 Crisp, white guardrails are a classic for a reason—they flatter most traditional-style homes.

Railing Kits and Systems

Nowadays, handrail and guardrail systems are a great way to add panache to what would otherwise be an ordinary deck. Manufacturers—particularly those of synthetic decking materials—have responded to consumers' growing desire for distinctive railings by creating easy-to-install railing kits. Some systems are as simple as a stack of bowed-steel balusters and a spacing tool to ease installation. Others offer preassembled balustrade panels that you cut to length and snap between specially extruded rails. Some builders mix and match, using preassembled balustrade sections set into conventionally framed wood posts and rails. For a lighter, contemporary look—and one that's less likely to block your view—consider guardrails made with stainless-steel cable or rods, tempered glass, or aluminum. Make sure they meet building codes in your area before you make your purchase.

❶

❷

3

1 Stainless-steel tubing and copper post caps are two options available with several composite railing systems.

2 Instead of solid-glass panels for guardrails, consider glass balusters. Slightly tinted versions create an entirely different look.

3 White guardrails and handrails, an option from several makers, look elegant. The kits often include post sleeves, hidden hardware, and decorative post caps.

4 These aluminum baroque-style balusters add a bit of the ornate, are relatively inexpensive, and are easy to install.

4

1. A guardrail that is part wall and part piping has a contemporary look, especially with the post capped in a matching color.

2. Metal balusters are available with ornamental turnings and castings, such as those shown here.

3. Vinyl railing systems may be better suited to houses on the beach; saltwater is harsh on metal, and constant UV exposure can be brutal for wood finishes.

4. For minimally obstructed views, consider stainless-steel cable rails. They are typically installed horizontally but can be done as vertical pickets if so desired.

5. Cables can be installed on your own wood or metal posts, or with aluminum post-and-rail systems supplied by the manufacturer.

6. Mixing wood and metal in your guardrails keeps your deck current without being too trendy. The bench/rail combo here breaks up the heavy lumber with thin metal balusters.

1

2

3

4

5

6

Skirts and Skirting

Skirt or fascia boards are typically 1-inch-wide trim pieces that may be used to hide rough framing, such as header joists. You can paint them to match your house trim or finish them to match the decking or railings. Run skirt boards under overhanging deck boards, or cover decking edges and ends for a flush look. They should extend an inch or two lower than the framing they cover. As wood-to-wood contact promotes rot, apply preservative and use spacers to create an air space between skirt boards and joists. An air space is not necessary when using synthetic trim boards over pressure-treated wood.

To hide the entire space between deck and ground, use skirting panels. Made with wood or composite boards, or with lattice panels, they help keep balls, pets, and other animals from getting under the deck. Lattice is available in both pressure-treated wood and vinyl. A solid skirt gives the deck a more massive, formal look, as if the deck were built on a foundation. Open lattice, either in a diamond or windowpane pattern, has a lighter feeling and allows ventilation (important in damp climates). Choosing to use no skirting panels will make the deck look as if it were floating—especially if you have cantilevered the joists and decking around the perimeter. (See illustration on page 211.) If you do opt for skirting, be sure to include one or more access doors to the space you're enclosing.

1 Skirting on the underside of a deck doesn't have to be made of lattice. Masonry, such as the brick shown here, offers a more substantial look.

2 Lattice panels are versatile enough for skirting and privacy screening, shown here, as well as for trellises and windbreaks.

3 Skirting isn't a problem with ground-level decks, but edges look better covered with fascia boards. These composite boards bend around deck curves.

4 Composite skirt and trim boards can be ordered in the same color as the decking. There's no need to match the color with stain.

5 Here, a composite is used for the skirt board and the rail cap, two deck parts that are vulnerable to rot.

④

③ ⑤

Smart Tip **Skirt the Skirting**

There's no rule about screening off the underpinnings of your deck with lattice panels or other materials. If you have the headroom but won't be using the space for storage, the area can be left open and be used as a shady retreat when the sun is high and hot. Decks that are a few feet off the ground can be screened with plantings, such as evergreen shrubs. Wisteria and other flowering vines can also be planted around the deck perimeter. They screen the rough framing beneath the deck and can be trained to grow up the balustrade to break up the rigid look of many decks.

Use plants, such as the wisteria and hostas seen here, in place of skirting to hide deck piers and beams.

Decking Size and Pattern

Decking is perhaps the most important visual element of a deck. It's most noticeable when you walk on it, but with low, ground-level decks, it can also be seen from the yard. As such, it can play a big role in how well your deck fits with your house and yard. While most decks are built with standard 6-inch-wide deck boards, consider narrower boards if they suit your house better. For example, if your house has siding that has been installed with a short exposure (the distance from the bottom edge of one course of clapboard or shingling to the bottom of the next course), 4-inch-wide deck boards may look better. The size of your deck is a factor as well. A small deck will look bigger and more interesting if you use narrow deck boards. Consider alternating wide and narrow boards to reduce the scale of the decking as well.

A decking pattern will generally "blend" with the house better if it runs parallel with the predominant lines of the house. Typically, this means running the boards parallel to the longest dimension of the deck. An added benefit is that exposed deck board ends will be limited to the short ends of the deck and therefore less visible.

For decks that turn a corner or are set at an angle to the house, consider running deck boards on a diagonal. Doing so makes the deck look like a single shape rather than a patchwork of several shapes. You may use deck boards to create decorative patterns as well. These tend to work best when echoing the shape of the deck, such as a large hexagon, but they can also serve as focal points that are unrelated to the deck shape. Composite boards can be easily bent to create quite elaborate inlaid decking patterns.

1

2 3

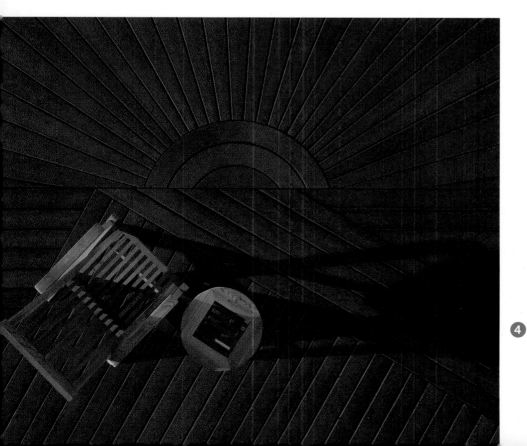

1 The unexpected serpentine decking pattern is in keeping with the climbing vines that flourish all over this architecturally intricate composite deck.

2 The composite decking, laid in the same octagonal pattern as the end of the house, reinforces the link between inside and outside.

3 Radiating boards in a polygonal deck draw your gaze out to explore views of the surrounding area.

4 With composite decking, your creations have almost no limitations, as this sunburst pattern shows. Often, however, simplicity works best.

4

Color Your Deck

Decks are far more colorful than in years past. Even composite materials come in dozens of colors and can be stained in dozens of others. For a formal look, match deck trim and guardrails to house trim. Finish decking with a solid stain or paint that matches the house siding. For a more rustic feel, approximate the natural colors of wood. For high-quality species, such as redwood, cedar, and mahogany, that may mean using a clear or transparent finish. For common species and pressure-treated woods, a semitransparent stain may achieve the desired effect. If perfect matching seems too boring, look for a hue that complements siding and trim colors. Natural clapboard siding, white trim, and light-gray decking, for example, is a popular combination. Climate, too, is a consideration. Dark colors in warm climates will likely make decking unbearable for bare feet in the summer, but too light a color will show dirt and mildew faster.

1 Color is "in," both indoors and out. When choosing colors for your deck, take cues from nature, as shown with these deep-red composite boards, or from colors used on your house.

2 This covered deck provides enough shade to keep these rich, brown composite planks cool from midday sun—a real concern if you opt for dark colors.

3 Painting remains the best way to add color and personality to your deck, as shown with this checkerboard pattern. The deck may have to be repainted every few years, but the impact is worth it.

1 Several recycled-plastic-lumber manufacturers make deck boards in colors such as tan, burgundy, blue-gray, and green.

2 Standard colors for composites most often imitate redwood, cedar, mahogany, and gray weathered wood, but other neutrals and exotic look-alikes are available.

3 Sky-blue railings and fixtures combine well with the Cape Cod gray of the composite decking.

4 Midnight blue is unusual for a deck trim and pergola color, but used here it complements the cedar shingle siding and decking.

1

2

3

4

General Deck Lighting

Adding light to your deck will allow you to enjoy it in the evening. You can, of course, opt for candles or torches, but electricity can't be beat for convenience. There are a wide variety of 120-volt and low-voltage fixtures available at home centers and lighting stores.

Make lighting the entrances from the deck to the house your first priority. Wall-mounted lights, such as sconces or lanterns, are available in styles that range from contemporary to Colonial. The fixtures should not be as elaborate as what you would use at a primary front door entrance, but try to choose something that works with the style of your home and deck—and that will not cause glare for you or your neighbors. When in doubt, go with a simple design. Some lighting retailers will allow you to borrow the fixture so that you can hold it in place and see how it looks.

Supplement wall-mounted lights with recessed lights in the eaves of your roof where it overhangs your deck. They offer an unobtrusive no-glare look but provide plenty of light. As a bonus, they accent interesting wall textures such as cedar shakes, stone, or brick. Other solutions include eave-hung or post-mounted lanterns. Entry lighting fixtures are often sold in collections, making fixture coordination easy. Finishes range from oil-rubbed bronze to pearl nickel and bright brass—some with low-maintenance finishes that are warranted for many years.

Your next priority should be to light the transitions to your yard. Low-voltage lighting is a good choice here. It requires transformers to step the household current down to 15 volts or less, but it is easier to install—no need to bury cables, for example. Wiring for low-voltage systems is much simpler, too, and there are fewer safety issues. Use path-lighting fixtures near the foot of stairs, as well as lights that you can recess in stair risers and mount on balustrade posts, to improve safety. You can read more about lighting on pages 174 to 177.

3

1 A strategically placed sconce can highlight deck details, such as the fine stonework of this outdoor fireplace.

2 Post-cap light fixtures add interest and light to an otherwise ho-hum guardrail.

3 When adding lighting to a deck, begin by adding light near the entrances to the house. Install wall-mounted lanterns for both safety and security.

1

Smart Tip **Before You Buy Lighting**

When purchasing outdoor lighting, check to be sure the fixtures are UL listed for use in wet and/or damp locations. Cast-aluminum fixtures will suffice for most applications, but fixtures made of marine-grade alloy aluminum, die-cast brass, solid copper, and rugged composites are the most durable. Look for porcelain bulb bases for durability, and be sure the fixture design makes it easy to replace a burned-out bulb. Options such as etched, seeded, or translucent glass help protect viewers from glare. Several manufacturers have introduced "dark sky" shield accessories to help avoid night-sky pollution and to enable compliance with night-sky protection ordinances that are being enacted around the country. Other features to look for include motion detection for saving energy (either built-in or as an option you can add on later) and energy-efficient compact fluorescent bulbs.

1 Illuminating the pool and spa, as shown here, is a great way to add light and drama to a deck.

2 Use several hanging lanterns to light an outdoor activity area, such as this covered dining space.

3 Recessed lighting can provide some much-needed light over a protected food-preparation area.

Chapter 5

Selecting Materials and Hardware

Designers and homeowners today have more options when it comes to deck-building materials than they did just a few years ago. Most new products have been aimed at producing decks that require less maintenance. The trend toward synthetic wood products is the most visible shift. Synthetics eliminate the need for annual sealing and often for refinishing.

Synthetics are not all that's changing the face of decks. A variety of blind fastening systems offers a cleaner look for deck surfaces. Under-deck drainage systems offer a drier environment below the deck. New textiles make shading systems less obtrusive and more versatile than ever before. Low-glare lighting fixtures increase the usefulness of decks, improve safety, and create delightful effects—whether viewed from the yard, deck, or house. Improved wood treatments no longer contain arsenic and make pressure-treated lumber safer for everyone concerned, from carpenters to children.

Once again, however, new materials change the way things are done. The copper-compound-treated woods demand fasteners with better resistance to corrosion. Moreover, steel connectors, such as joist hangers, must be protected from direct contact. The old wisdom of buying high-quality materials, however, remains as true today as in the past. Decks, as previously noted, take abuse—even more than roofs because they're subject to foot traffic as well as the elements. Better materials will keep your deck looking good longer.

Vinyl planking and railings stand up well to the elements and cost about the same as the best woods.

Traditional Wood Varieties

There are three types of untreated wood commonly used for decking: redwood, cedar, and cypress. Redwood ranges in color from light to dark red, has a handsome straight grain, and takes finishes well. Heartwood redwood is resistant to rot, decay, and insects. The drawback to redwood—and it's a big one in many parts of the country—is the price. It's often four times the cost of pressure-treated wood. To save money, consider using redwood for only the visible applications and using pressure-treated pine or fir for structural components. Be aware that without staining every one to two years, redwood fades to silver.

Cedar decking (typically western red cedar) has many of the same qualities as redwood but costs significantly less. It is lighter in color and less red than redwood, weathers to a pleasing gray, and is distinctively fragrant. The heartwood offers rot- and insect-resistance. Cedar lumber is as easy to work with but softer than redwood. For structural members, be sure to use grades rated for strength, such as select structural or No. 1 structural. For a contemporary deck, opt for the custom clear grade; for a rustic look, choose a knotty grade. Like redwood, cedar takes finishes better than heavier woods, such as southern yellow pine.

Bald cypress is less well known except in its native regions, such as the American Southeast. The trees flourish in swampy areas, hence the wood's natural resistance to rot and insects (heartwood only). Prices vary, depending on how far you live from cypress's natural habitat, but remain

1 A garden grade redwood, as opposed to an architectural grade, is used for decking. Choose one of the heartwood grades, such as deck heart (shown here), for applications where wood is on or near soil. Use a sapwood grade, such as clear or B grade, for decking where there is a low likelihood of insect or decay problems.

2 This seaside deck, constructed from custom-clear grade western red cedar, will weather to a light gray and blend perfectly with its surroundings.

3 Cedar decking will likely show wear patterns if painted or stained. Paints and opaque stains can, however, be used on railings, as shown on these guardrails.

affordable in the Southeast. Cypress lumber does not readily absorb water and takes a long time to dry once moisture is absorbed. Therefore, it is less dimensionally stable than redwood or cedar and needs to be dried carefully prior to use to avoid twisting and warping. When new, the color ranges from tan to red. It weathers similarly to cedar.

All three types of wood work well as decking, but heartwood is expensive and often unavailable. Lumber harvested from new growth, lighter in color and called sapwood, may not have the same resistance to insects and decay. If you do find a source for heartwood, be sure it's a reputable, certified dealer so that these resources are not over-harvested.

❸

❷

The Exotics

Just looking at photos and hearing claims of maintenance-free, long-lasting wood decking is enough for many homeowners to consider installing an Ipe (aka Pau Lope, ironwood, or Brazilian walnut), teak, Brazilian cherry, or Philippine mahogany deck. All of these woods benefit from being extraordinarily dense and rich with natural oils. This makes them extremely resistant to decay, fungal growth, wood-boring insects, and even fire. Ipe, for example, is twice as strong as oak and more durable than redwood. The downside to being so solid is that saws and drills have a hard time penetrating many tropical hardwoods. Expect additional labor costs for predrilling, additional blades, and so forth. Exotic woods will cost more before labor, too—about the price of redwood. There is no doubt about exotic wood's beauty, but don't count on its staying its just-milled color without some maintenance on a par with what you'd need to do for cedar or redwood.

❶

❷

1 Hardwood decks, such as this one built of Brazilian Ipe, require little maintenance and are durable.

2 Exotic hardwoods do have some drawbacks. They generally require predrilling and countersinking prior to driving the recommended stainless-steel fasteners, which adds expense.

3 Ipe has many attributes, including the highest ratings for durability, and insect- and fire-resistance.

4 This deck, built of Cambara mahogany, is about 5 years old and shows no signs of checking, cupping, or splintering.

❸

❹

Pressure-Treated Wood

For most homeowners, pressure-treated (PT) lumber is the most cost-effective and practical deck-building material. Available species include pine, hemlock, and fir, with southern pine and Douglas fir being the most common. PT wood is extremely resistant to rot and insect damage. The process involves placing wood in a vacuum chamber filled with liquid preservative. Varying degrees of penetration determine how the lumber is graded. Wood rated for aboveground use, for example, has less preservative than wood rated for ground contact.

Today's PT lumber processors have replaced arsenic with copper compounds, such as alkaline copper quaternary (ACQ types B and D) and copper azole (CA-B). The new formulations pose no known threat to humans but may affect marine life. Copper compounds are, however, highly corrosive to other metals, so hot-dipped galvanized or stainless-steel nails and screws are recommended for fasteners. Steel-framing hardware, such as joist hangers, must also be shielded from contact with ACQ- and CA-treated wood, typically with a self-adhering membrane. PT wood color ranges from dark greenish-brown to light brown, and it can be stained or painted once it's dry. Newer PT products are about 10 percent more expensive than arsenate compounds, but the improvements in environmental and human safety are worth the extra cost.

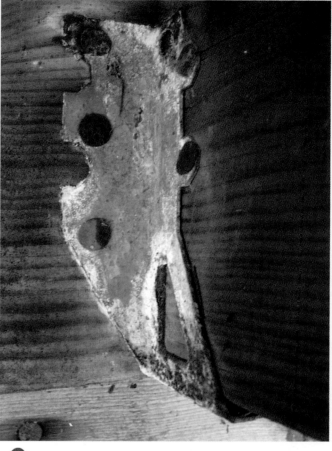

1

2

1 The corrosive effects of the new types of copper-based wood preservatives are evident on this joist hanger.

2 Use self-stick shielding membranes, shown here, or hot-dipped galvanized framing hardware and fasteners to avoid corrosion problems.

3 This new type of pressure-treated wood was introduced to the market recently. A solution of nontoxic sodium silicate is driven into the lumber, which is then baked. The result is a PT wood that does not corrode connectors and fasteners.

4 This deck, built of pressure-treated southern pine, will remain good-looking for many years with regular cleaning and occasional refinishing.

❸

Smart Tip **Out with the Old**

CCA (chromated copper arsenate) pressure-treated wood, its safety rarely questioned for 70-odd years, has been removed from the market. Concerns about arsenic leaching from lumber in decks, playgrounds, and other applications prompted investigations by the Environment Protection Agency (EPA) and other environmental groups. The studies' results were mixed, but CCA (and other compounds with arsenic) in pressure treatments is no longer available for most residential uses. The EPA has not, however, called for removal of CCA-treated lumber in existing structures. If you're concerned, a penetrating oil finish or paint will reduce or eliminate exposure to CCA in older decks.

❹

Synthetic Deck Materials

Some synthetic products, called composites, combine wood fiber and plastic, often reclaimed from wood waste and recycled plastics. Others are made from vinyl. Both are primarily used for decking, but many manufacturers also offer matching components for guardrails and handrails. Synthetic trim boards and moldings are also available. Neither composites nor vinyl materials are recommended for structural components, such as joists, posts, or beams.

Synthetic products have some advantages over the real thing, as well as some drawbacks. They are not subject to rot or checking and won't splinter. They come precolored, so they don't need finishing upon installation. Some types are easier to bend, lending themselves to extraordinary railing designs and decking patterns. Synthetic wood's big selling point is that it requires less maintenance than wood.

You don't have to seal it every year to keep it looking good.

On the other hand, synthetic lumber products are expensive—often as much or more than top-quality wood products. Despite cosmetic improvements, synthetics don't quite look or feel like wood either. Some brands are not as easy to work with as wood due to their weight and density. Composites will "weather" (fade or turn gray) and need to be refinished if you want to maintain the original color. Dense types of synthetic lumber hold more heat than real wood, causing discomfort when walking with bare feet. They also get dirty, can stain and scratch, and will support the growth of mold and mildew—though not as readily as wood. Although it can be argued that synthetic lumber saves natural wood resources, some are not environmentally friendly and are a source of hazardous pollutants during their manufacture. (See "Greenest Decks," page 116.)

1 Newer composites mimic the look of expensive exotic woods, such as this Ipe on the left and Cambara on the right.

2 With composites readily available in different shades, you can install inlaid patterns on decking as if it were an interior hardwood floor.

3 Composites trump real wood when it comes to installing sweeping curves on a deck; these boards are easily curved around the pool.

❶

②

③

Smart Tip **Do a Test Drive**

Not all composite boards are created equal. Some accept fasteners cleanly, without mushrooming or breaking the end grain. Others don't. Ask your supplier for recommendations, or take home samples and check them out for yourself. While you're at it, check for resistance to stains and scratches as well.

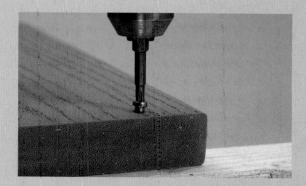

Mushrooming—having a bump over the fastener head— is a rare occurrence with newer composite boards.

③

④

1 One type of vinyl decking, this plank version, is installed similarly to composite products with biscuit joiners.

2 Another type is a slide-and-snap installation, in which boards clip together and are self-spacing.

3 Composite planks with grooved edges, such as this product, make no-show-fastener installations easier.

4 Standard white vinyl railing systems coordinate well with most composite and vinyl decking.

115

Smart Tip **Greenest Decks**

It used to be that building "green" was a luxury, or even considered an eccentricity, but those days are over. Rising energy costs, air and water pollution, and, some say, even global warming are real, and the building products industry is beginning to respond to consumers' growing concern for the environment. Decks are no exception.

Wood is the natural "green" deck-building product. It's biodegradable, produces few if any toxic byproducts, and is usually renewable. It can, however, have negatives for the green builder. Tropical wood decks, for example, increase demand for products harvested from rainforests, causing poor countries to sacrifice irreplaceable resources for quick profit. Even in North America, demand for redwood, cedar, and cypress can outpace responsible supply.

Be a conscientious consumer and seek out lumber sources that are certified by the Forest Stewardship Council (which operates worldwide) and the Sustainable Forestry Initiative (only in North America). These organizations regulate forestry operations to promote prompt reforestation, efficient wood utilization, and protection of water quality and wildlife habitats. Consumers can search for certified dealers (Forest Stewardship Council only) and get more information about lumber labels on the organizations' Web sites, www.fscus.org and www.aboutsfi.org.

Some experts consider recycled plastic lumber (RPL) a green option, too. RPL includes many composite and some all-plastic products, but check the percentage of recycled material and type of plastic before you buy. The Healthy Building Network (www.healthybuilding.net), for example, rates several well-known manufacturers of composite products as "less environmentally preferable." Some plastics, including vinyl and polystyrene, create human health risks during manufacturing and have limited options for recycling. Products that recycle hard plastic (polyethylene) are environmentally preferable. RPL also has a higher price tag than most wood, but this is somewhat offset by its low maintenance. A not-so-green aspect of composite RPL products is that they're not biodegradable and cannot be separated back into plastic and wood waste.

❶

❷

❸

Aluminum Decks

Underutilized, but attractive and with some unique benefits, aluminum decking is likely to gain market share in the future. It is low maintenance, lightweight but strong, prefinished, cool to walk on, recyclable, and has a clean, contemporary look. It's also substantial enough so that denting and noise are not problems. Built-in channels between the planks carry away rain, so no additional under-deck drainage system is needed should you want to put a patio below an upper-level deck or use the space for storage. Aluminum decking is well suited to harsh seaside climates and for use with roof decks. Matching aluminum guardrails and handrails are also available.

1 Recycled plastic lumber that uses no wood fiber is easier to break down and use again and can look great in the right setting, such as this Spanish-style house.

2 Aluminum decking can easily be mixed with wood railings and other wood structures. These red metal balusters and post caps, for example, combine with white aluminum decking to create a refreshing look.

3 Interlocking aluminum planks form a waterproof surface, keeping the space below dry.

Plywood Decks

Plywood decking is another alternative to using solid-wood or synthetic planks. It has a more formal, less busy appearance than traditional decking products. Waterproofed properly, it provides a dry space below. One system involves caulking and taping all joints and then rolling on several coats of acrylic polymer. Once cured, it forms a flexible but tough skin on the plywood that is suitable for normal deck traffic. Granules can be added to the last coat to add texture and improve skid resistance. Ideal for creating a deck over a flat roof, this product also can be used to weatherize a traditional wood deck. A second system achieves roughly the same effect but with a heavy vinyl membrane that you roll in place. The seams are overlapped and heat-welded. Likened to an outdoor sheet vinyl flooring, it's available in various colors, patterns, and textures.

1 You have several ways to waterproof a plywood deck. This homeowner did it with fiberglass, resin, and marine paint, similar to the way you would treat a boat hull.

2 If you think a plywood deck is déclassé, check out the dining deck on this custom home. Coated with an acrylic polymer, it is relatively easy to apply. (See next page.)

Applying an Acrylic Polymer Finish

1 To apply an acrylic polymer deck coating, all joints must first be sealed with caulk.

2 Smooth caulked areas with a trowel so that they are flush.

3 To ensure watertight joints, embed joint tape in polymer as specified by the manufacturer.

4 Mix texture granules into the deck coating for a slip-resist-ant surface.

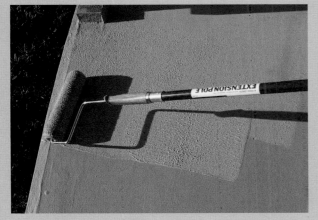

5 Apply two thick coats to the entire surface.

6 The cured coating offers a tough finish with a pebbly texture.

Posts, Beams, and Piers

In most deck designs, footings, beams, and joists are normally hidden. Good thing, too. The standard lumber and hardware used in most projects is often nothing to look at. Some designers and architects, however, see the deck's underpinnings as an opportunity to show off. They believe that good design should show the logic of the structure. Others have no choice. The support structure of upper-level decks and decks built on terrain that slopes away from the house will be exposed to view no matter what.

   In such cases, you have several options:

- **Accentuate beams** by extending them beyond the deck perimeter and cutting the ends with a distinctive profile.

- **Clad piers, posts, and columns** with wood, brick, or stone. This is especially effective when the house also includes these materials.

- **Craft posts from full logs** or rough-hewn timber. Either one will look better than standard milled lumber.

- **Use less-obtrusive diagonal braces** in place of posts. Check with your local building department to be sure they meet building codes before you begin.

- **Use decorative deck hardware,** such as column caps and joist hangers. They are offered by the same companies that make standard framing hardware and typically come powder-coated in black.

1 Assemble posts from several pieces of lumber to add mass and to make columns proportional to the volume of the structure.

2 The structural supports to this deck are meant to be seen.

3 Cantilevering a deck, here with the assist of diagonal bracing, is a good way to minimize the visual impact of a deck's underpinnings.

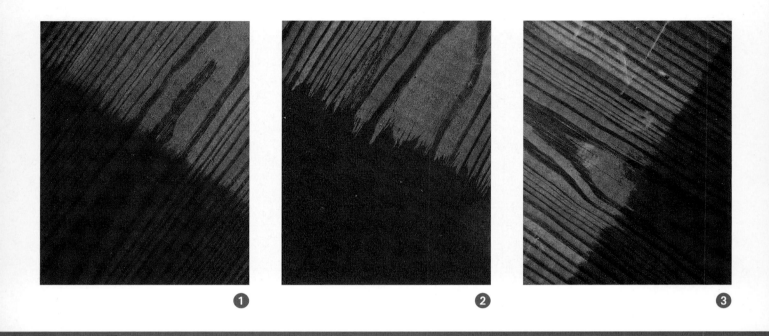

Finishing Options

If you are wondering why you can't use just any finish on your deck, think about the abuse decking must handle, including pounding rain, snow, and ice, abrasion from traffic and furniture, and often many hours of direct sun, day after day. To make matters worse, the joints between the many parts of a deck retain moisture long after the rain stops, making the wood vulnerable to rot, mildew, and wood-munching insects. To combat this barrage, deck-finish manufacturers offer a variety of formulations that include sealers, preservatives, UV-light inhibitors, pigments, and resins. Some are oil based and penetrating. Some are acrylic and film forming. Others are a mix. Here is a list of the most popular finishing options for a new deck:

• **Clear sealers, or water-repellent preservatives,** are the most popular choice for new decks. They help protect wood from moisture, thereby saving it from repeated cycles of soaking up water and then drying out. Unprotected, wood will crack, warp, cup, splinter, and check. Sealers must be reapplied regularly to remain effective, but even then, the wood will weather to gray. Water-repellent preservatives contain a fungicide to fight mildew.

• **Toners, or transparent stains,** offer more protection than clear sealers. They deepen and enhance the color of the wood, and the grain remains visible. You can use these finishes on pressure-treated wood to approximate the look of more expensive woods. The best products in this category penetrate the wood surface, protect it from damaging UV light and mildew, and leave a substantial top layer to resist moisture. They are relatively expensive finishes but will retain the original color of most woods if applied strictly according to the manufacturer's directions.

Note: Exotic hardwoods like Ipe or mahogany are dense with natural oils and don't absorb penetrating stains as well as softer woods. Allow them to weather to a teak-like gray, or treat them with a hardwood-specific finish according to

1 Use a cedar toner, also called a transparent stain, to simulate the look of more expensive decking.

2 If it's solid color you're after, your best option is an opaque stain.

3 A penetrating oil with UV protection, such as this one, will enable you to retain the natural wood color—at least for a while.

4 Semitransparent stains are available in a variety of hues, including the moss green shown here.

5 Clear sealers, often combined with preservatives, protect wood from moisture penetration.

the manufacturer's recommendations to maintain the original wood color.

• **Semitransparent stains** generally have more pigment than transparent stains and do a better job of hiding imperfections and unattractive grain patterns. Alkyd- and oil-based versions excel because they penetrate the wood better than acrylic formulations. All are available in a wide variety of wood tones and colors.

• **Solid stains** are more heavily pigmented than semitransparent stains. (Think thinned paint.) They offer superior protection against UV rays and hide the color and grain of the wood. They, too, come in a wide variety of colors. Oil-based products usually last longer, but water-based formulas are easier to clean. Expect wear patterns to show in heavily-trafficked areas.

• **Deck and porch paints,** unlike many stains, are film-forming products. This makes for superior UV and moisture protection, and is great for camouflaging lesser grades of lumber—but paint may blister and peel, and will eventually show wear in high-traffic areas. Use paint if you want a bright gloss or semigloss finish to match or complement paint on your house exterior. Acrylic- and alkyd-based paints are available and should be applied over an oil-based primer. Mix the paint with clean sand to improve slip resistance if desired. Keep painted decks swept free of dirt (it wears finishes away faster), or place outdoor carpets along traffic paths to prevent wear. Sand and recoat as necessary.

• **Preservatives** prevent fungal growth, rot, and decay—and some also protect against wood-boring insects. They are recommended for treating untreated wood as well as the site-cut ends of pressure-treated lumber. Preservatives alone are not finishes. They may, however, be sold in combination with sealers to provide moisture protection as well, making them a one-step finish. Some preservatives can be used prior to applying paint for added protection against rot and decay.

Buying Lumber

Buying lumber and boards (the distinction being that boards are less than 2 inches in nominal thickness) is not just about choosing one species over another. There are a number of other factors to consider, including moisture content, grain, grade, and even what part of the tree the material comes from. Minimize warping, shrinking, and insect infestation by buying lumber and boards that have been kiln or air dried so that the moisture content is less than 19 percent.

When possible, choose wood cut from near the center (heart) of the log. The grain will be vertical, narrow, and close. Lumber from the outer portion of the log is likely to have grain that is flatter, wider, and V-shaped. Narrow grain is generally more attractive and better at taking finishes. Lumber where the grain is close to parallel to the long edge will be stronger than wood with grain that runs diagonally to the edge.

Grading systems vary, but most lumber and boards are available in at least one "select" grade and several numbered common grades. Select grades are nearly knot free and are reserved for applications where visual appearance is paramount. The higher the grade number, the more knots and defects and the bigger the knots will be—and the more likely they will affect strength. Most decks are built with No. 2 common grade lumber. Be sure your lumber choices adhere to local building codes for deck construction.

The grade stamp that's printed on just about every piece of lumber and board will indicate grade, species group, moisture content, and the grading agency.

Smart Tip **Heartwood vs. Sapwood**

All trees have heartwood, the older, denser wood near the center, and sapwood, the wood closer to the perimeter that brings sap to branches. Species like pine and fir aren't usually graded on this basis because so many younger, faster-growing trees are felled today. However, the distinction is made for redwood and cedar because attributes such as insect- and rot-resistance apply only to the heartwood. Both species have many grades, from architectural (the best and most expensive) to utility. In general, use better grades for visible deck components, such as decking and rails. Use construction heartwood grades near soil, or use less-expensive PT lumber. As there are so many grades, you may want to inspect the lumber before taking delivery. Spending a little extra time now will prevent disappointment later on.

❶

A Primer on Fasteners

Most experts recommend screws rather than nails for installing deck boards and assembling guardrails, stairs, and support framing. But that's only half the battle. Selecting the right screws depends on the decking material, the look you want to achieve, and the environment.

New pressure-treated woods, for example, are corrosive to common steel. You must use either double hot-dip galvanized steel, ceramic-coated, or stainless-steel fasteners. All are available with epoxy-coated heads in colors selected to blend nicely with commonly available deck materials.

Many exotic woods, because they are so long lasting, deserve stainless-steel fasteners. Although they're more expensive, they will last the life of your deck and not leave corrosion stains around the heads of the fasteners.

Composite decking accepts most screws but forms a "volcano crater" around the driven screw head. You can pound down the crater with a hammer, hiding the screw head. Alternatively, use specially designed ceramic-coated or stainless-steel screws that install cleanly in one step. They are colored to match the deck and nearly invisible when installed. Composite wood tends to be extremely hard, so it is best to use screw heads that are square driven.

If you are near salt water or in a cold, wet climate, a marine-grade stainless steel (type 305 for inland decks or type 316 for the seashore) will show no corrosion—even after years of exposure. Note that stainless steel is softer than steel, so a more substantial screw is often needed or you may break off screw heads while installing the screws—and probably mar your decking while trying to extract them.

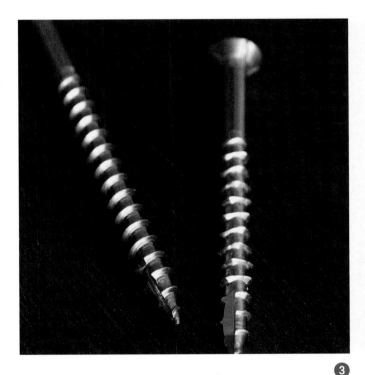

1 These flat, sawed boards show the orientation of annual rings. Most builders install decking bark-side up. The theory is that if boards cup when wet, water will drain rather than pool. Many builders, however, install boards with the best-looking face up. Talk with your builder to be sure you take all variables into account.

2 Stainless-steel screws are available with colored heads to match the color of your decking, making them nearly invisible.

3 New stainless-steel screws are designed for penetrating hardwoods and composites without the need to predrill.

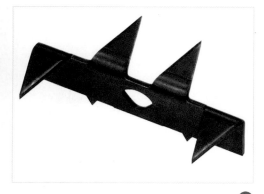

Hidden Fasteners

Blind or hidden fasteners will give your deck a clean look. They will also make your deck easier to clean and eliminate the possibility of staining due to fasteners, which is sometimes a problem with top-down installation. Hidden fasteners, especially those that install with screws from below, minimize the number of penetration points in decking and joists, a leading cause of wood decay.

Biscuit-type blind fasteners are preferred because they can be installed from the deck surface. (You don't have to crawl below the deck.) They do, however, require a biscuit joiner to make the requisite slots in the plank edges at each joist—a time-consuming process. Some blind fasteners can be installed from the deck surface and do not require a biscuit joiner—the fasteners' sharp metal prongs are simply pressed into the board. Be aware, however, that this is not always an easy task in hardwoods and composites.

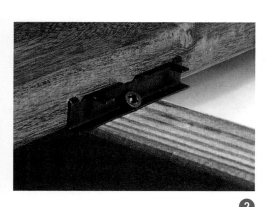

1 With one style fastener, sharp prongs are pounded into the plank edge.

2 The fastener is then screwed to the joist.

3 Blind fasteners are available for both wood and composite decks, such as the one shown here.

Installing Biscuit-Style Blind Fasteners

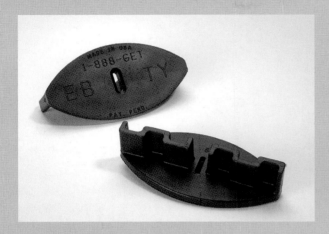

1 Biscuit-style blind fasteners, such as the ones shown here, require some special tools to install.

2 The first board is screwed in place. The fastener is counter-sunk and plugged.

3 A biscuit joiner is used to cut slots in plank edges where they intersect with joists.

4 The biscuit is inserted into the slot. Thanks to a spacer built into the biscuit, spacing between planks is automatic.

5 A screw anchors both the biscuit and the board to the joist.

6 A special wrench is used to make deck planks snug.

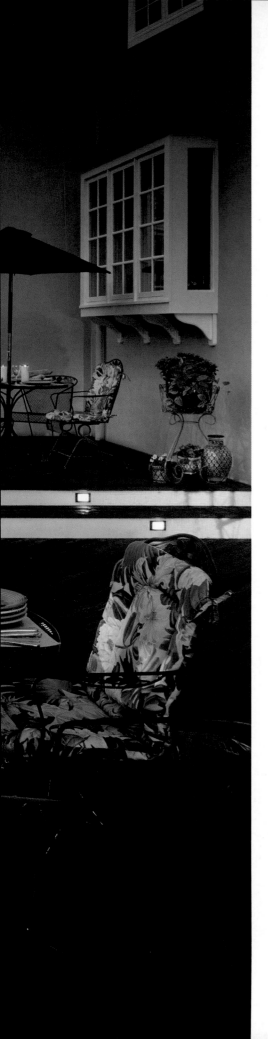

Chapter 6

Build It Safe and Sound

When one thinks about deck safety, it's normally in terms of structural practices and good workmanship. On upper-level decks, for example, an improperly installed ledger board (the board that attaches one edge of the deck to the house) could pull away and cause a catastrophic accident. A poorly anchored guardrail could also spell disaster. Even a carelessly installed fastener can lacerate bare skin.

However, design decisions can make a big difference, too. Where decking levels change—at a platform, for example—alter the decking pattern or paint the riser to signal the step. Otherwise, under poor lighting conditions, a visitor may take a spill. If you choose a dark color for your decking but it gets too hot during the dog days of summer, lay light-colored outdoor carpeting in high-use areas to prevent foot burn (not to mention splinters). Made of polypropylene, new products look just like sisal or jute carpets but are nearly impervious to the weather. They are also quite easy to clean. Just pull them off the deck, and hose them down.

Position through-deck features, such as fire pits, garden beds, and ornamental ponds, where they will not become tripping hazards. Good places include adjacent to deck level changes (but not steps), alongside on-deck planters, and next to privacy screens. If the opening is near traffic, install railings. To enjoy your deck in safety, review these hazards—as well as those in the following sections—with your deck designer and builder.

Lighting, especially at minor level changes and around seating, can improve your deck's safety at night.

Permits and Codes

A building permit, issued by your local municipality's building department, will typically be necessary for any structure that requires footings. You will be required to submit your deck plan, pay a fee, and abide by relevant building codes. Building codes govern all aspects of deck construction and will have a big impact on your design, so it's good to be aware of them. Your town building inspector will enforce them. Some building departments will give you a handout, outlining the codes. Many others will not. State building codes may be purchased online in book or CD form. They are expensive, so try your local library first. Building codes will define everything from how far your deck must be from property lines and the street (setbacks) to details as minute as fastener size, composition, and placement.

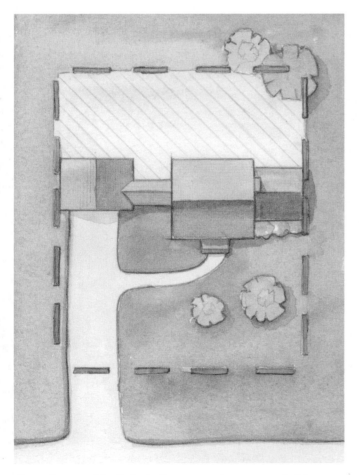

Above Your municipality typically governs where you can build on your property. For example, you may not build a deck beyond the setbacks at the the front, back, and sides of your yard (shown as a dashed line in the illustration above). Nor may you build within the prescribed setback to a septic field.

Smart Tip **Safe Landing**

Allow ample space for landings at doors. You should not have to step backward off a landing in order to open a door. Small landings, unless used with sliding or in-swinging doors, are hazardous—especially when carrying food and supplies to the deck. Preferably, the platform for a door that swings out to a deck should be 2 feet deeper than the door width.

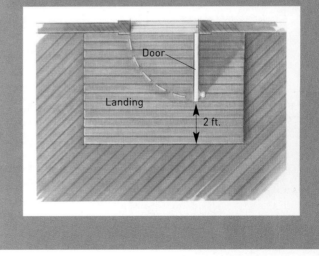

1 Portable fire pits are a great compromise for those who want to enjoy an outdoor fireplace on cool nights but don't have the space or budget for a built-in. Make sure your fire pit has a screen to protect guests and the deck from sparks, and use with extreme caution around children.

2 Grills, which are pretty much a prerequisite for decks, also must be used with caution. Find a place for your grill that is convenient but out of the way of normal traffic and that is at recommended clearances from railings and house siding.

Lighting for Safety and Security

If you plan to use your deck during the evening, consider installing safety lighting at steps and along deck perimeters that have no guardrail. General lighting, either around the deck perimeter, on posts, or attached to the house, will also help prevent accidents due to trips and falls. (See "General Deck Lighting," page 100.) Many outdoor lighting manufacturers make safety lighting products designed especially for decks. Some install directly in stair risers or stringers. Others go under railings or atop balustrade posts.

To illuminate a sizable deck and the yard beyond for reasons of security, floodlights—house-, pole-, or tree-mounted—are a good solution. Look for models that offer motion detection and energy-efficient lamps, such as compact fluorescent or metal halide. Some models will wirelessly activate other house lights and/or sound a chime inside the house when someone is approaching. Other floodlight models include a motion-activated, wireless color video camera. Be sure to avoid positioning floodlights in ways that will cause glare to your neighbors.

2

3

1 Lights for every step and obstacle make this elaborate deck much easier to navigate at night.

2 A winding staircase can be treacherous in the dark, so consider adding some simple rail lights.

3 Use a specialty drill bit, shown here, to make holes for the stair-riser light fixtures.

4 Low-voltage lighting fixtures, such as this one, are easy to install—but seek advice from the manufacturer about the transformer size you'll need for your layout.

4

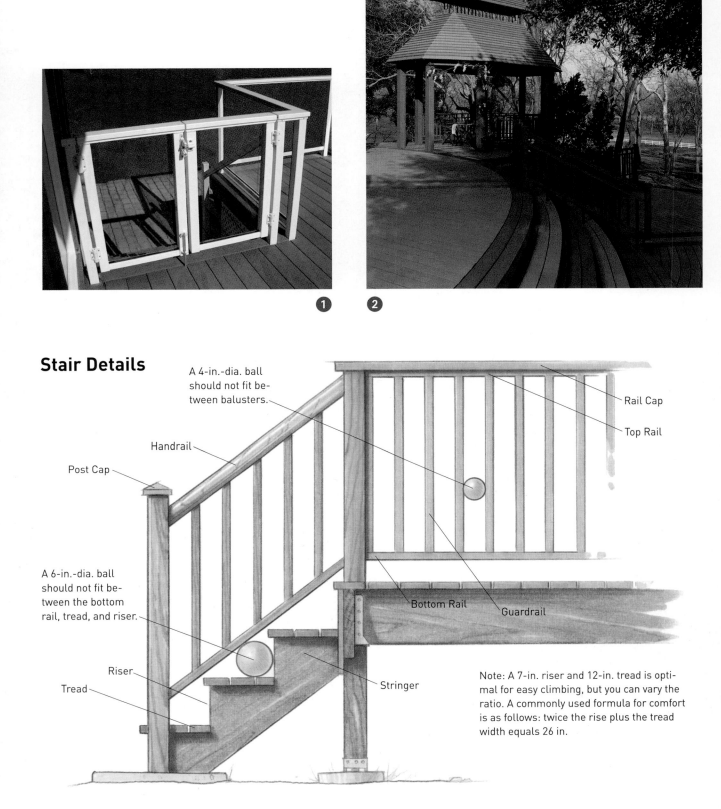

❶　❷

Stair Details

A 4-in.-dia. ball should not fit between balusters.

Handrail

Post Cap

Rail Cap

Top Rail

A 6-in.-dia. ball should not fit between the bottom rail, tread, and riser.

Bottom Rail

Guardrail

Riser

Tread

Stringer

Note: A 7-in. riser and 12-in. tread is optimal for easy climbing, but you can vary the ratio. A commonly used formula for comfort is as follows: twice the rise plus the tread width equals 26 in.

Safer Stairs

Your state and local codes will define stair variables, including handrail requirements, riser height, stringer width, and baluster spacing. In general, you will need handrails for any stair with more than three risers. They must be fully graspable and between 34 to 38 inches high, as measured from the tread nosing. The maximum riser height is typically 8 inches and the minimum tread width is 9 inches. Typical combinations include 6- to 7-inch risers and 10- to 12-inch treads. For safety, wider treads are better. For comfort, the rule of thumb is that twice the riser height plus the tread width should equal 26 inches. The narrowest dimension for a stringer (the wide, angled board that supports stair risers and treads) is usually 3½ inches. Baluster spacing is the same as it is for guardrails: less than 4 inches. Many building codes also limit the number of steps in a single run. (You can't fall as far if you trip.)

1 This glass-paneled gate matches the deck railings and is an ideal solution for homes with young children.

2 Although these steps with ample treads are easy to negotiate, the homeowner added a handrail for safe access, which is usually a requirement for stairs with more than three risers.

3 Handrails should be fully graspable for maximum stair safety, as shown here.

3

1

2

1 Built-in fireplaces are generally a safer way to have a fire on your deck than an open fire-pit dish. Gas-fired flames are usually safest of all. Regardless of what you choose, check with the manufacturer for safety procedures and clearance recommendations.

2 While trees incorporated into a deck need a bit of wiggle room, the gap between trunk and deck boards can become a hazard. Consider installing a wrap-around bench to avoid any accidents.

Deck Safety Checklist

Inspect your deck upon its completion and at least once every year thereafter. Here are the hazards to look for and what to do about them if you find them:

Splintered Decking. Sand the affected areas and reseal. If splintering is extensive, cover the deck with outdoor carpeting until you can replace (or turn over) the boards. Today's outdoor carpets look remarkably like carpeting woven from natural fibers such as sisal and jute. They are available at home centers and flooring stores.

Loose Balusters. Wood balusters are typically toenailed between the top and bottom balustrade rails. Resecuring a loose balustrade may simply be a matter of driving the fastener deeper with a hammer and nail punch. If the nail is still loose, replace it with a slightly larger diameter screw.

Protruding Nails or Screws. Use the appropriate tools to sink fastener heads below the surface of decking and rails. If still loose, replace with deck screws as required.

Rotted Stair Treads or Decking Boards. An awl is a good tool for finding rot and insect damage. If it sinks into the suspected board easily, remove the board (where possible) and replace it. If rot or insect damage is found in a structural member, call in professional help.

Loose Ledger. Using a flashlight, check for evidence that the ledger has pulled away from the house. If you suspect the ledger has pulled away slightly, seek professional help with the repair.

Level Joists and Plumb Posts. Use a 4-foot level to see if decking or posts are out of level. If they are, it may mean that a footing has shifted or sunk. Call in professional help if this is the case.

Applying sealer annually will help keep decking splinter-free. Installing decking that has been seasoned, such as this western red cedar, will help prevent splintering as well.

The ledger is the backbone of your deck, so make sure it is securely fastened with no signs of corrosion or rot.

Whether to Build It Yourself

Building a deck is often portrayed in magazines and books as being a project that's within the ability of most home-owners. While that may be true for small, ground-level decks, only experienced do-it-yourselfers need apply for a deck of any size or complexity. The toughest aspect of building the average deck is locating and installing the footings and piers (masonry supports, similar to footings). You may want to enlist someone with experience for this task. You will also need a strong person to help you move and install long beams and joists. Owning a table saw and knowing how to use it will be very helpful, especially when making repetitive cuts for balusters. A drill/driver with extra battery packs is essential for fastening decking to joists. The rest of the job is straightforward, until you begin building the stairs. Precut pressure-treated stair stringers, treads, and railing components, available at home centers, will, of course, speed the job and make it easier.

Anatomy of a Deck

Building a deck is not a project for a beginner. Even a small, simple deck, such as the one illustrated here, requires an understanding of construction basics.

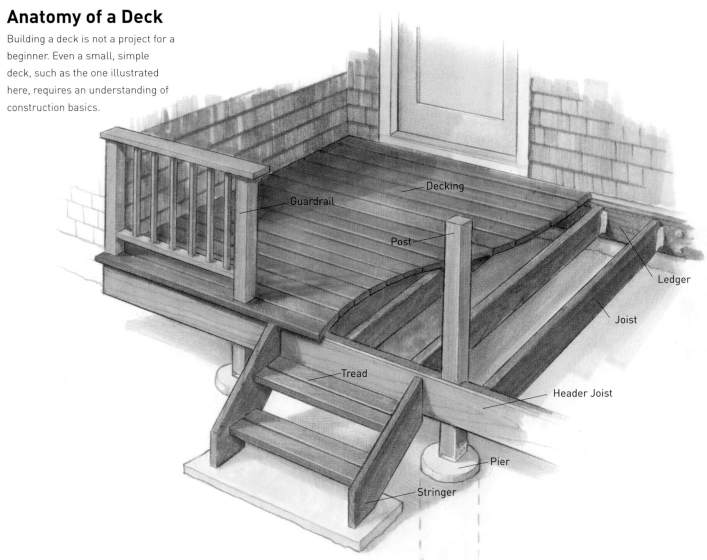

Ledger Details

Understanding the importance of flashing and fastening the ledger to the house is critical for anyone who is contemplating building a deck.

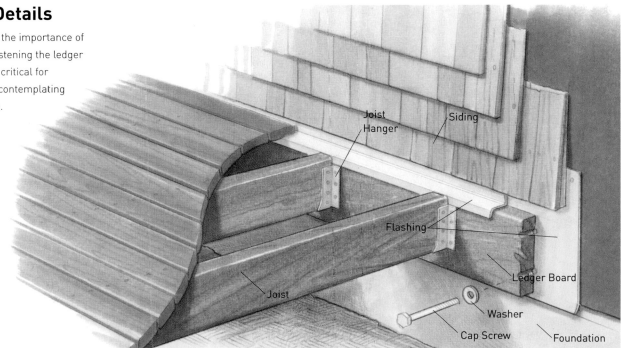

Smart Tip Reusing CCA

If you're remodeling an old deck, it's OK to leave in place or reuse CCA (chromated copper arsenate) pressure-treated lumber, assuming it's in good condition. Although now banned due to the arsenic used in the preservative, it is unlikely to be a health issue. Wear a dust mask, however, when cutting or sanding it, and don't use it for a food-preparation counter or a play structure. Discard sawdust and scraps according to your local laws. Never burn it, because that is the best way to become exposed to the arsenic.

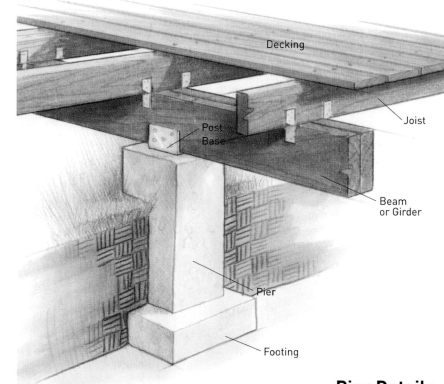

Pier Details

Pouring a footing and pier precisely where you need it is a job that requires you to have experience—or know someone who does.

Part 2

Get More From Your Deck

Chapter 7

Raise the Comfort Quotient

Your deck may look terrific and be in just the right spot, but if it's not comfortable, its use will probably be limited. Comfort has several dimensions, including protection from the elements (wind, sun, and rain), control of annoyances (insects, noise, glare, and temperature), and ergonomics (well-designed furniture, stairs, and storage).

Sometimes the solutions are simple. A well-placed wall, for example, can buffer sound and wind. A few yards of shade cloth can reduce sun and glare. Solving other problems is not so easy and may involve adding an entire structure to your deck, such as a screened-in gazebo.

There are comforts of a less physical nature as well. Privacy, for example. You don't want to feel as though you're a fish in a bowl every time you step on your deck. A trellis or arbor may be the solution, or a solid balustrade—or it may be as simple as drawing a shade. (See page 156.) You may also want to create a sense of security that has nothing to do with

any real threat. Small, cozy areas come to mind. They bring big spaces down to a human scale. Reserve a small "room" on your deck and enclose it with potted and climbing plants, if that appeals to you. Add a fountain to drown out the noise from passing cars. Set up your outdoor speakers; sit back in your favorite lounge; and enjoy your retreat.

In this chapter, we'll explore solutions to both physical and psychological discomforts in hopes that you can borrow the ideas for your deck.

Shade is a key for comfort. This umbrella, which can tilt and rotate, does the job. See the following pages for other options.

Wind Screens

Controlling wind, especially if you live in an area where it blows much of the time, is one of the more tricky deck comfort problems to solve. That's because wind does not always act as you would expect it to. A solid wind barrier, for example, may cause wind to curl over the wall and swirl at you from behind. The solution is to build your wall so that some wind will filter through. A wall built with a lattice panel set into the upper section is one option. Spacing the boards of a fence or wall an inch or two apart is another. Designers often use tempered (heat-treated) glass panels set atop guardrails to reduce wind as well. Thicknesses range from ¼ to ½ inch and are typically set into commercially available aluminum guardrail systems. Outdoor fabrics can be effective as well, as long as you don't mind the flapping sound when the wind gets gusty.

1 Tempered glass panels installed over a solid guardrail offer stiff resistance to wind without blocking the lovely view.

2 Breaking the wind with boards that are staggered and gapped, like the ones on this composite pool fence, minimizes turbulence on the leeward side.

Shade Umbrellas

Keeping a sunny deck cool during the hot months is no easy task, but creating some shade will definitely help. The simplest approach is a center-post umbrella that's designed to fit through a hole in a dining table and into a base below. If you go this route, buy a large umbrella that's 8 to 12 feet wide and easy to open and close. Octagonal units will give you more shade than square units of the same width. You'll want a heavy base to keep it anchored when the wind blows. Alternately, buy a base that bolts to your deck, assuming one position will handle your deck's changing shade patterns.

Side-post umbrellas get the post out of your way and come in even wider sizes. The umbrellas mount on an arm or hang from a boom that can rotate 360 degrees to block the sun as it crosses the sky. The most expensive units have a tilting mechanism. Check with your manufacturer's instructions to ensure secure deck mounting in windy conditions. No-post umbrellas can be hung from an overhead structure, such as an arbor or pergola. Such units are raised and lowered using a pulley.

Outdoor fabric choice is about looks, durability, and light transmission. There are several types on the market, including acrylic canvas, PVC fabric, and high-density polyethylene (HDPE). Acrylic canvas and PVC are best for water resistance, but HDPE is best for blocking UV rays in hot, arid climates. Typically, however, the best UV-ray-blocking HDPE is not water resistant. Some fabrics are treated to resist mold and mildew, too.

❶

❷

③

1 If you decide to use a center-post umbrella, choose one that tilts for maximum effectiveness.

2 Side-post umbrellas allow flexibility when arranging deck furniture—and eliminate the need to talk around the post during dinner parties.

3 If you have a pergola, you can hang your umbrella, eliminating the post altogether.

147

Other Shade Devices

Shade sails, aptly named because they look like sailboat sails, are an innovative way to add shade and contemporary styling to a deck. Held together by stainless-steel cable sewn into the edges, the triangular or rectangular sails attach to posts or to the existing structure with steel rings at reinforced corners. Consult with a professional to find the sail configuration best suited to your climate and needs.

If you have a pergola or arbor structure, consider a retractable canopy. It discreetly installs along tracks on rafters, providing shade without interfering with the style of the structure. Deck awnings are another shade option. Manually or electrically powered, they attach to your house and provide protection from both the sun and the rain. Freestanding gazebos, fitted with outdoor fabric, will also offer some respite from the sun. Lightweight units offer portability, while heavier structures are semipermanent and may require special support framing or their own footings. Either can be fitted with drapes for privacy and screening for insect protection.

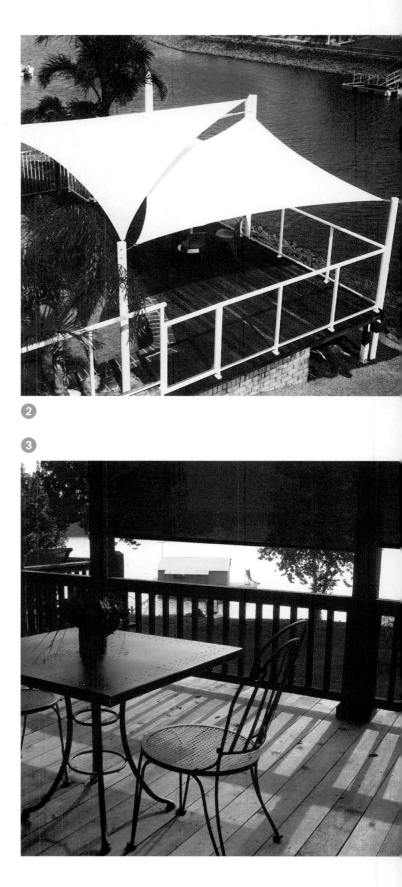

1 Shade cloth cut in long, triangular panels spans from post to eave for shading a large area.

2 Premade shade cloth panels, cut in interesting shapes, are available with varying degrees of translucency.

3 Shade cloth can also be hung vertically and used as outdoor shades, as shown here and on page 156.

Screened Enclosures

Screen houses or screen enclosures let you enjoy your deck even during peak seasons for flying insects. Models come in many different sizes in order to cover nearly any deck. You can also opt to cover only a portion of your deck. Models are either freestanding or three-sided, attaching to the house on the fourth side. Many are sold in kits for do-it-yourself installation and can be installed in as little as a single afternoon.

The best units have heavy-gauge aluminum frames with a baked-on enamel finish. Less expensive units have galvanized steel framing that's finished to resist fading and oxidation. Roofs are often constructed of vinyl fabric in a wide range of vinyl grades and thicknesses, from 6- to 22-ounce weights. Heavy-duty versions will handle moderate snow loads and have aluminum roofs with polystyrene insulation. If considered a permanent structure, as some are, you will need a building permit. Lighter-duty roofs should be taken down during winter months.

①

1 This permanent screened room covers the entire deck and was built for entertaining and family dining.

2 Without collar ties (rafter-to-rafter cross members that are typically used to stabilize an attached structure such as this one), the ceiling is open and unencumbered. Slats, spaced about ½ in. apart, hide the rafters. The stainless-steel rods, seen at the end wall, keep the structure from wracking.

3 This permanent screened room occupies one end of a long deck, offering shelter when the weather or the bugs get bad.

2

3

1 Eventually, the climbing vines will make a lush covering atop this pergola.

2 This deck, located in a warm climate, boasts two porches: an open-air one for barbecuing and a screened-in one for year-round use.

3 This screened room includes a fireplace that takes the chill out of the air on cool evenings.

1

2

3

153

Privacy When You Want It

The problem with privacy walls is that in addition to blocking the view of your deck, they block the view from your deck. A roll-up deck shade allows you to have complete privacy when you want it and a view when you don't. It's also ideal for situations where a solid privacy wall between decks (such as with a duplex or town house) would block a desirable view for your neighbors. As a bonus, the shades can serve as a wind screen.

2

1

3

1 Loops of elastic cord hold these deck shades in both the up and down positions.

2 The blinds offer both privacy and wind protection when rolled down, as shown.

3 When the shades are rolled up—a process that takes less than five minutes—the view is nearly unobstructed.

Smart Tip **Make Your Own Shades**

This design couldn't be simpler. Extend guardrail posts to the height desired for privacy. Then make shades from weather-resistant shade cloth to suit as shown. To raise the shade, roll from the bottom up and secure with elastic loops. Use elastic loops to secure the shades to hook screws in the down position.

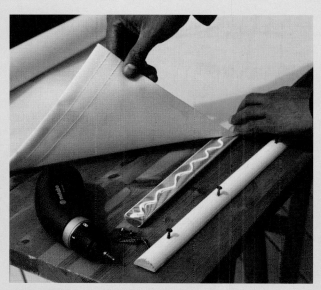

1 Fashioned from outdoor shade cloth, the shades are reinforced by sandwiching the bottom edge between two half-round trim pieces. Secure with caulk and screws.

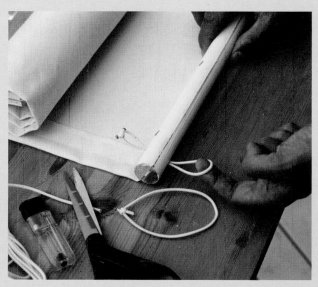

2 Bore two holes through the glued-up half-round. Then thread the elastic loops through the holes; tie them off; and melt the cord ends to prevent unraveling.

3 The shade top, reinforced with two flat pieces of trim, receives two loops of elastic that hold the rolled shade in the up position.

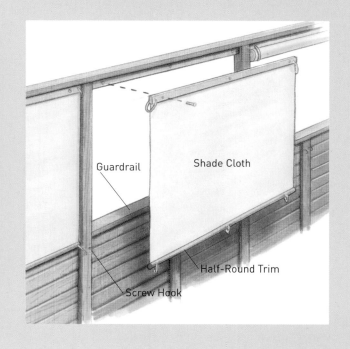

Guardrail

Shade Cloth

Half-Round Trim

Screw Hook

157

Gazebos and Other Deck Structures

If you're planning to build a trellis, arbor, gazebo, or other deck structure, it may be wise to incorporate it into your deck plan from the start. Otherwise you may end up with a yard that looks like a theme park, with too many unrelated structures. Even if you don't plan to build it right away, you can save yourself time and money later by anticipating your future needs now. For example, a large gazebo or arbor is likely to need extra footings and supports if you plan to build it on your deck. A shed may be able to be built under a section of the deck. Support for a hot tub or spa will almost invariably need to be engineered into your plan, and it's a lot easier to handle sooner rather than later.

If you're adding a structure to your deck plan, look to your home's architecture for inspiration. Existing soffit brackets, cornice moldings, and fascia widths all offer design guidelines. Try to mimic roof configurations and angles, too. Matching your home's trim color will also help blend the structure to the house.

Opposite This arbor has nearly disappeared under a cascade of roses. The wrought-iron furniture completes the look of this cozy retreat.

Arbor

Trellis

1 Pergolas, such as this one with scalloped lattice panels, provide both privacy and shade.

2 Even before the vines begin their climb, this arched trellis frames the patio door and adds some relief to a two-dimensional facade.

Pergola

1

2

1 Lattice panels on the ceiling and kneewall give this gazebo an old-days garden feel—and camouflage the plywood ceiling and diagonal bracing.

2 The lattice kneewalls also reinforce the insect screening where it's most vulnerable and match the deck skirting and yard fencing for a unified look.

3 Gazebos are ideal for detached decks; this one, assembled from a kit, offers a peaceful retreat—and a pretty focal point for the yard.

2

3

163

Chapter 8

Outfitting Your Deck

Furnishing and accessorizing your deck is fun. You have an array of products from which to choose, from furniture to fire pits. Be careful, however, not to go overboard—or all of the hard work spent getting your deck design right will go for naught. Put too much on your deck and it will become an obstacle course.

Priorities should include comfortable, versatile seating, adequate surfaces for serving meals, convenient grill placement, and storage for the items you'll want at hand (cushions, charcoal, children's toys, etc.) but that you don't necessarily want to look at all the time. If you intend to use your deck at night or year-round, you may also want to investigate outdoor lights, patio heaters, and fire pits.

Traffic across and circulation around your deck is also critical. Using accurate dimensions, plot your furnishings and accessories on graph paper before buying them. Allow at least 4 feet between items such as chairs and planters. Allow more space around grills and fire pits. Draw in paths that are likely to be heavily trafficked, including from house to yard, house to grill, and house to spa. Keep these paths at least 4 feet wide and clear of obstructions.

Only if you have the space should you consider extras, such as spas and decorative water features. These features require careful planning and substantial amounts of space, not to mention their own electrical circuits and weight support. If you haven't planned for such features ahead of time, they probably have no place on your deck.

Simple and serene, this deck accommodates a portable spa and two seating areas, one outdoors and the other screened in.

Deck Furnishings

Decks are just like interior rooms when it comes to furnishing them. You'll want to consider style, material selection, and scale to achieve the overall feeling you're after. Deck styles range from country rustic to island exotic— and so do deck furnishings. Wood tends to be best suited to the former, wicker and wicker look-alikes to the latter. But there are many choices in between. Wrought iron and cast aluminum complement traditional styles. Furniture of painted steel and aluminum tubing are more contemporary looking.When placing furniture, consider its function, views you want to show or hide, and traffic patterns. Dining sets for small gatherings are best placed in areas where there is no through-traffic. Avoid situations where guests have to pull their chairs in every time someone walks by. A separate dining area, such as an alcove, is ideal. It can be designed into the shape of the deck or created by positioning a planter or trellis to enclose the area. Even a decorative banner or drape hung on a cable can create a cozy effect. The dining table should, however, be easily accessible from both indoor and outdoor food-preparation areas.

If you plan large gatherings, such as a neighborhood barbecue, consider designing your deck with several seating areas rather than one large area. The secondary dining spots should be big enough for chairs and small tables to hold food and drink. Sometimes wide, flat, built-in benches can serve as overflow eating areas, acting as both seat and table.

❶

1 Multiple seating areas make this deck perfect for entertaining large groups.

2 Furniture that echoes an aspect of the deck, such as how the seat backs here closely match the balustrade, creates a pleasing fit.

❷

Design Tip **Choose Fitting Furniture**

Choose furniture that suits the scale and size of your deck. Massive pieces will overpower a deck with a delicate balustrade. Finely-wrought furniture may look lost on a large deck built with heavy timbers. Another pitfall is to put too much furniture on your deck. Whenever possible, choose pieces that are multifunctional. For example, a bench that can store cushions below, or chairs that adjust from sitting to lounging positions, will save you precious deck space.

Expand your search—indoor furniture, such as this bench, can look charming in the right outdoor setting.

Building Deck Furniture

Building outdoor furniture is not nearly as demanding as building indoor furniture. You don't need sophisticated tools or skills; finishing is simpler; and the materials are less costly. In fact, outdoor furniture can often be built from leftover deck-building materials.

This space-conserving, multipurpose furniture system is a good example. Consisting of three modules, it can trans-form from bench to lounge to chair. The modules can also serve as side tables. Two of the modules have a fixed top. On the third, the top is hinged to allow varied seating positions. To keep the modules from shifting while in use as seating, lock them together at the legs with hooks and screw eyes. The units may be left natural and treated with a clear preservative sealer, or they may be finished with stain or paint. Use cushions to improve comfort.

Left and Below Three modules easily convert from table and bench to lounge or chair. The ensemble is ideal for a small deck where there isn't space for a lot of furniture.

Modular Deck Furniture

1 For a lighter look, taper the legs using a circular saw or saber saw; then assemble the legs and rails as shown.

3 Assemble the adjustable top with 1¼-in. screws, waterproof glue, and wide cleats.

Right The furniture module with the hinged back is shown here. The other module is identical except that the hinged brace and notched rails are eliminated, and the slatted seat is screwed in place.

2 Assemble the fixed tops with 1¼-in. screws and narrow cleats; then fasten to rails as shown.

4 Attach the brace to the adjustable top with galvanized hinges and stainless-steel screws.

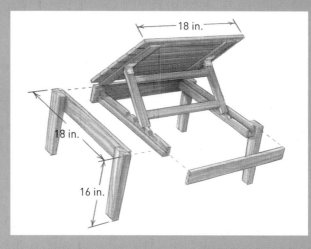

18 in.

18 in.

16 in.

Deck Storage Ideas

Decks, like most rooms, have a way of becoming repositories for garden tools, plant pots, cooking paraphernalia, cushions, and toys. Unfortunately, deck space in most situations is going to be limited. The last thing you want to do is use it for storage space. When designing your deck, however, keep storage in mind. Opportunities for storage are likely to arise, often in nooks and crannies that are not good for much else.

There are two basic types of on-deck storage: vertical mini-sheds, also called backpack or lean-to sheds, and horizontal sheds or deck containers. The former have small footprints, often only 3 x 4 feet. They're versatile though, able to unobtrusively nestle in the jog of an exterior wall. With a typical height of 6 or 7 feet, vertical sheds are efficient for storing garden tools, such as rakes, spades, shade umbrellas, and stacks of chairs. Vertical sheds may be wood- or steel-framed or all vinyl. With many vinyl units, the floor is integral with the walls and the sides are prefitted with supports for optional wood or metal shelving.

Horizontal sheds are large bins that resemble oversized weatherproof footlockers. Normally utilitarian in nature, they are generally made of vinyl and designed to be unobtrusive for fitting in odd spaces, such as under a raised deck, under

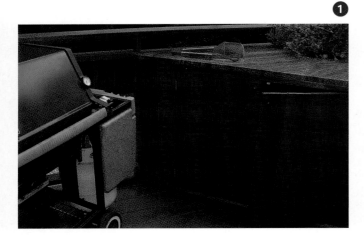

a work surface (such as a potting area), or beneath deck stairs. Most units open to the front as well as the top for easy access and cleaning. A typical size is 3 x 4 feet and 3 feet high, big enough for a trash barrel and some garden supplies or a mower with folding handles. Large units have an interior capacity of about 45 cubic feet. Long garden tools, such as rakes, may not fit.

Not all horizontal sheds are utilitarian-looking. Finely crafted wooden boxes, called patio or deck boxes, can be used to store cushions, umbrellas, and folding chairs and are quite attractive. They can also be fitted out with coolers, condiments, and dinnerware for convenient alfresco dining. Some units incorporate shelving or removable trays, and some can double as a bench or serving table. Lacking the budget, building a similar deck storage box from leftover decking materials is a relatively easy project.

1 Built-in cabinets, such as this one topped with granite, are handy places to store grilling materials and to prepare foods.

2 This portable storage bin serves as a table, with wings that fold open left and right.

3 An on-deck, portable cabinet can hold everything from sunblock to chair cushions. This cabinet is made of teak to resist moisture.

4 Even a ground-level deck can offer plenty of storage below. This one has room for four kayaks.

❹

Smart Tip **Building an Under-Deck Shed**

For decks at least 42 inches high, plan to use the below-deck space for storage. Keep the area dry by installing an under-deck drainage system. (See page 218.) Items you can store include outdoor power equipment, such as mowers and snow blowers, as well as hand garden tools. Store kayaks and canoes on brackets hung from joists. For storage areas with low head clearance, put items on a wagon or in a cart so that you can pull them in and out easily. Other storage candidates include bicycles, firewood, and bulky garden supplies. It's a good idea to include several doors so that you can access stored materials from several points around the deck perimeter. Below-deck storage is also perfect for patio furniture, umbrellas, and grills during the off-season.

1 The space below a raised deck offers lots of storage possibilities if you incorporate a roof or drainage system to shed water. Here, the space is used for potting.

2 Below the other end of the same deck, the space is used to keep firewood dry and accessible during inclement weather via a basement door.

3 This large deck houses an array of power equipment and a workspace below. Skirting boards are staggered to hide shed contents but do allow ventilation.

❶

❷

Decorative Lighting

Add decorative lighting to set the mood on your deck. Possibilities are endless, from low-voltage commercial strings woven along balustrades or in nearby branches to fixtures that hide in your hanging planters. Adding lights to your yard will greatly enhance the view from your deck at night, create drama, and make you feel more secure. Choose from up-lights and spotlights (often used to accent trees and sculpture), spread lights for throwing light horizontally across a garden bed, and wash lights for revealing texture on a surface, such as a masonry wall or chimney. Up-and-down lights, mounted in a tree, create a moonlight-like effect. Outdoor decorative lighting fixtures are available in both line and low voltages and often with a choice of lamps, including incandescent, halogen, and compact fluorescent. The latter are energy efficient and longest lasting. Avoid solar-powered lights because their light output is very low.

1 Many designers feel that outdoor lighting should be seen—but the fixtures shouldn't be. The designer of these posts subscribes to this notion. By day they have unassuming post caps.

2 At night low-voltage lamps, hidden under the caps, distribute a soft glow across the deck.

3 Some outdoor lighting fixtures are meant to be seen, such as this nautically-themed lantern.

1

2

Smart Tip **LEDs on Deck**

LED lighting fixtures are the future for low-voltage deck and landscape lighting according to industry experts. Such lights are already being used on deck stairs, in balustrades, and for post lights. Past problems with the bluish color and weak output have been overcome. The big advantage to LEDs is they have a life of 50,000 hours—or enough so you'll never have to change a bulb again. Although LED-lit fixtures cost more than traditional ones in the short run, they're cheaper over the life of the fixture. In addition to lower maintenance, LEDs conserve electricity and are cooler, so the lens won't burn curious little fingers.

❸

❶

1 These simple, contemporary-style post lights create an interesting light pattern but are shielded to prevent glare.

2 Choose light fixtures that look good even in daylight, such as this windowpane cover with a shell-like lens.

3 Recessed fixtures work best for a clean-lined and contemporary deck.

4 This Arts and Crafts-style sconce highlights the texture of railing boards while generating interesting shapes of light.

5 Look beyond your deck; highlighting surrounding trees, rocks, or sculptures with spotlights can change the visual focus after the sun goes down.

2

3

4

5

Spas and Hot Tubs

Spas and hot tubs are wonderfully relaxing, but making a splash on a new deck shouldn't be taken lightly. Carefully work out the details of spa construction, size, the number and placement of water jets, location on your deck, and support well before any concrete is poured or framing is built. Spas are available in many materials, from acrylic to stainless steel and ceramic tile, and in sizes that fit up to seven or eight people. Water jets, in a myriad of configurations, provide hydro-massages.

You'll want the spa in a location that maintains privacy and stays out of the way when entertaining, without feeling isolated. Often, a separate open-air or screened gazebo works well, while providing a convenient space to store robes, towels, books, and shoes.

If the spa is part of the main deck structure, consider installing built-in seating around it and using planters to separate it from other activity areas. Spas may be installed flush with the deck or can be "portable" and sit on the deck surface. Flush-mounted spas usually require a concrete slab for support, while topside installations need beefed-up framing and extra footings. Spas will also need a water source, electrical service, housing for pumps, valves, and filters (if not already built into the unit), and a ground fault circuit interrupter (GFCI) to prevent possible electrocution should water and electricity meet. Consult with a licensed electrician and plumber about these issues early in the design process.

1 Flush-mounted spas are the least obtrusive, whether you're preserving a scenic view of the ocean or of a more typical backyard. They do, however, require access from below for servicing.

2 The stone surroundings of this spa contrast beautifully with the western red cedar of this deck.

3 If you choose a spa that sits atop your deck, look for an attractive cabinet that will blend with your decking material.

4 In a small yard surrounded by neighbors, create a private corner using vented privacy walls such as these.

❶

2

3

4

1

1 Water features, such as this ornamental pool and "waterfall," help make this simple deck a tranquil retreat.

2 In wide-open spaces, going below grade is sometimes a way to find the privacy you want. The stone retaining wall and ornamental pool provide perfect opportunities for rock and pond gardening.

3 Create your own water views. The homeowners can enjoy this ornamental pool from both deck levels.

2

Ornamental Water Features

Ornamental water features can't massage your back, but they do provide relaxation and can buffer unwanted noise. Fountains are either freestanding or wall mounted. Both will require a power source to run the pump's motor, and you should add water occasionally to replenish the system and keep the pump functioning well. If the fountain has a large water basin, consider using a direct water source and a float valve to maintain the water level automatically. Again, you may need to consult a professional plumber.

Small ponds and reflecting pools are most often permanent structures with poured concrete or brick bases. Water must be kept aerated to prevent algae growth, so you'll need a pump. Pumps need a power source, so a GFCI is once again necessary. Pools and ponds can be lined with either a rigid or flexible liner to keep water from draining; stones around the edge keep it in place and add a natural look. Pools and ponds open up many opportunities for gardeners because mail-order nurseries offer vast arrays of unusual aquatic plants, such as water lilies. You can even enjoy fish— just be sure to keep the raccoons away.

❸

Grill Areas and Outdoor Kitchens

Decks are used for grilling more than anything else. Even during the off-season, many families enjoy cooking outside. Portable grills should include side tables for resting serving plates. They should also have wheels so that they can be moved out of the way when not in use. Choose a unit that doesn't drag the propane cylinder when you move it—or you may gouge your decking. Today's grills include many convenient features, including larger cooking areas, easier-to-clean stainless-steel grates, long-lasting brass and stainless-steel burners, and extras like side burners and rotisseries.

For a seamless look, built-in grills are an option. Many grill and range manufacturers sell them. Advantages include permanent gas hookups (liquid or natural gas), larger grilling areas and roasting capacity, optional burners and rotisseries, and durable weatherproof construction. The downside, of course, is the same as with all built-ins—don't plan on changing your mind about where they're located. If built of stone or brick, you may need to provide extra support below deck. Built-ins are expensive, too. The basic grill units start at $1,000 before adding in accessories, construction materials, or labor.

Regardless of whether you go with a portable or permanent grill, consider adding a portable or permanent food-preparation and staging counter close by. Use the space below the counter as a cabinet for basic cooking and serving supplies. Makers of built-ins offer door assemblies that match the grill construction. A lower-cost built-in option is to build a "docking station" for your portable grill. Build flanking cabinets and countertops to either side. Put the cabinets on locking castors if you want portability. Use water-resistant finishes and exterior-grade plywood, and be sure to observe grill-to-wood fire-prevention clearances as recommended by the manufacturer and codes. Polished stone, stainless steel, or porcelain tile are good choices for the countertop material.

1

1 No more canceled barbecues. This cooking and dining terrace stays dry thanks to the deck drainage system above.

2 Deep eaves protecting a portion of your deck are a big plus, but unless you're building a new home they are difficult to incorporate.

3 This large deck offers plenty of space for gathering around the cook—without getting in the way.

❷ ❸

❶

1 Adding a sink with hot and cold water is the ultimate for an outdoor kitchen; it puts cooking, food prep, and cleanup all in one place.

2 With lots of space, you may choose to keep some distance between diners and the grill.

3 On a compact deck, you may not have a choice about where to put the grill. Here, it puts the chef in a traffic lane—but with this view no one's complaining.

❷

❸

Fire Pits and Fireplaces

A built-in fire pit is a wonderful feature to have on your deck, assuming you plan to use it often. Otherwise, however, it consumes a lot of space, presents some safety issues, and can be an eyesore much of the rest of the time. If you only plan to enjoy fires five or six times per season, consider a chimenea or portable fireplace instead; portability will allow you to clear your deck for other activities. The latter unit, often called a fire bowl and ringed with a stone ledge, doubles as a place to set down a drink or plate. After each use, you will want to dump the ashes. (Add them to your compost; they are a great fertilizer.) A safer and more convenient option, albeit a less romantic one, is a gas-fired fire pit. Safest of all is a built-in masonry fireplace. It can be tucked close to the perimeter of a deck, so it won't take up a lot of space, and can be used for grilling. The flue will help keep smoke out of the eyes of you and your guests. Clad with stone or brick, it can be made to complement materials around your house and yard.

Regardless of whether your fire fixture is permanent or portable, observe codes and follow the manufacturer's clearance recommendations. Some portable units are not recommended for placement on decks without installing a fireproof barrier.

❶

❷

❸

Smart Tip **Patio Heaters**

Patio heaters are not just for your favorite outdoor cafe anymore. More and more homeowners want to extend the outdoor entertaining season on their deck using these parasol-shaped heaters. Heaters come, of course, in other shapes and sizes, but these seem to be most popular because they are movable. They can be found at outdoor furniture stores and on various online shopping sites, and they average about $300. Be sure to read the info on what type of fuel the heater takes (kerosene, butane, propane, or natural gas) and the radius of heat it will project. The patio heater should also include various safety features such as emergency cutoff valves, flame controls, electronic ignition, and even infrared heating technology. Whichever model you purchase, place it in a wind-sheltered area that's small enough for it to effectively heat. Keep children a safe distance away.

1 This fire pit—the centerpiece of a semicircular seating area—has plenty of clearance around it yet stays out of the way of other deck activities.

2 Gas-fueled options such as this fire pit are generally safer for decks than a portable fireplace but will need to be connected either to a propane tank or a natural-gas line.

3 Electric mountable heaters are convenient and are easy to keep out of the reach of curious children.

4 Prior to using any patio heater, do a maintenance check on the gas hose and other components according to manufacturer's instructions to avoid potentially dangerous accidents.

❹

Chapter 9

Deckscaping

A deck offers a great vantage point from which to enjoy your yard, but don't forget that in most cases, for better or worse, it also becomes the focal point of your home landscape. As such, it is important to design a deck that complements instead of dominates your yard.

Border plantings, trees, and on-deck planters all help to integrate this multilevel deck and yard.

Previous chapters have discussed the importance of borrowing architectural details from your house as a way to keep a deck from looking as though an alien spaceship has docked itself to your back door. Use the same approach to make a connection between your deck and yard, but this time by allowing elements from the yard to intrude on your deck. A sure way to accomplish this is to use some of the same plants growing in the yard on your deck. Clumps of irises or tulips on and off the deck, for example, would do the job nicely. For a longer-lasting effect, make room for an island bed of perennials or shrubs that are prevalent in your yard. Suitable perennials include hosta, false spirea, day lilies, sedum, yarrow, and peonies. Compact shrub speci-mens, such as dwarf spruce, spreading juniper, holly, lilac, ornamental grasses, and ornamental quince, offer a bit more mass and staying power. Dwarf ornamental trees offer the best long-term solutions.

You can also use nonplant materials, such as large stones, a water feature, or a yard sculpture, to naturalize your deck. If you're planning to include an outbuilding or play structure in your yard plan, it too may be an opportunity for creating a deck-to-yard link. Be sure to use complementary materials and colors. At the very least, use planters and trellises to bring greenery to your deck. In this chapter you'll find specific ideas that will help you have a deck that shows off your green thumb instead of one that sticks out like a sore one.

Integrate Deck to Yard

Ground-level decks and multilevel decks that step down to near grade level are the easiest to relate to yard and gardens, especially if you've allowed for garden islands or planters. The task is made simpler by not having to contend with obtrusive balustrades or staircases (although your local building codes may still require a stair railing at the point of egress). If your deck is rectilinear, and you want to maintain a formal look, choose border plants that mimic it, such as a hedge of holly, yews, or boxwood. Hedges provide a good transition to the yard and a foil for other, more colorful plantings. They can be grown in almost any scale. If your deck is boxy and you want to soften its edges, try training vines to grow along the skirting and guardrail. A few wisteria vines, for example, can quickly envelop a large deck and turn it into a private retreat; however, they will need pruning several times a year. An upper-level deck may benefit from tall trees planted nearby. Fast-growing firs, arborvitae, and pines will all draw attention from (or hide) ungainly support posts—and may provide some privacy, too. Just don't plant them where they'll eventually block a desirable view. Don't plant trees too close to your deck, either, or droppings from birds and the tree itself will add to your list of chores. For a long deck that's 3 to 5 feet off the ground, choose trees that grow laterally instead of straight up, such as a Japanese white pine or Korean dogwood.

1 Big rocks, plants, and planters all conspire to make this outdoor-shower deck a part of the sylvan yardscape.

2 The organic shape of this composite deck integrates it physically and visually with the compact lot's trees and shrubs.

2

191

Design Tip **Vary the Depth**

When designing the landscape around your deck, your intention should not be to screen out the yard but to create an interesting view. Unless privacy is a problem, plant trees and shrubs at varying distances from the deck for a view with depth and interest.

1 This terraced garden serves to connect the deck to the yard by acting as a secondary set of stairs and as planters.

2 Annuals, such as these zinnias and cosmos, make good plantings around a sunny ground-level deck. Try new combinations the following year to vary your view.

1

2

Deck Planters

There's no easier way to integrate your deck with your yard than with planters. Deck planters typically take the shape of boxes or large pots. When buying or building the former, try to match the materials, colors, and board dimensions of the deck. While not critical, doing so will help make the planter blend in better. For large plants and beds, it's best to build your deck around an island garden so that roots have direct contact with the ground. (See examples on page 198.) This is of course easier to do with ground-level decks, but it can also be done with decks that are 2 or 3 feet off the ground if you construct a large, raised bed.

Deck gardens are ideal for herbs. Plant containers can also be teamed with trellises to create living privacy screens, or placed or hung on railings to soften the look of a balustrade. Choose varieties that bloom at different times of the season so you will always have color.

1 This curved built-in planter adds color and greenery to the deck and directs traffic safely away from the step-down to the deck's lower level.

2 This planter also forms the back of a long, built-in cedar bench.

3 A spreading juniper and large rocks help ease the transition from yard to deck here.

4 A large, portable planter box, such as this ready-made unit, can also act as a safety barrier at the deck's edge.

Choosing Planters

For a formal deck decor, use several containers of the same shape. Mix in a contrasting shape, such as an urn among rectangular planters, to create a focal point. Use planters and pots in a variety of shapes and colors for a more informal approach. Plants in large containers and pots are easier to keep watered than plants in small ones—the soil will not dry out as quickly. A layer of mulch over the soil will reduce the need for irrigation, as well. Planter materials include wood, terracotta, glazed ceramic, and plastic. Each has advantages and disadvantages. Wood planters can be built to match the materials and trim details of your deck for a coordinated look. Line the inside with building paper or sheet rubber to protect wood that may be subject to rot. Reddish-colored terracotta planters have a rich, warm look—especially handmade ones—but may crack if subject to freezing temperatures. Glazed ceramic pots offer some freeze-resistance and are a great way to add color to your deck but are heavy to move about. Plastic pots, especially those made to look like terra-cotta, look nice, insulate roots, are lightweight, and rarely crack in freezing weather. Nevertheless, they still have a plastic look about them and are subject to gouges.

1 These planters were hung on the privacy wall, conserving deck space and putting flowers at eye level for easier weeding and watering.

2 A mix of multilevel decking with on-deck and in-ground planter boxes makes this deck feel at one with the landscape.

3 Rail-riding planters bring flowers to where you can better enjoy and care for them.

❶

❷

Rail Planters

Rail planters or balustrade boxes keep decking free of clutter and are simple to make. Build several and fill them with herbs or your favorite annuals. A planter, such as the one shown below, can be made from scrap wood and a couple of dozen nails or screws. Be sure to bore drainage holes in the bottom along the outboard edges so the rail doesn't stop the water. It's also a good idea to place two small spacers under the box to permit ventilation between the planter bottom and railing. Or you can opt for a liner. If so, buy the liner first and use it for determining your planter dimensions. Cut holes in the liner to align with the drainage holes in the base of the planter. This will prevent the soil from becoming boggy after a heavy rain.

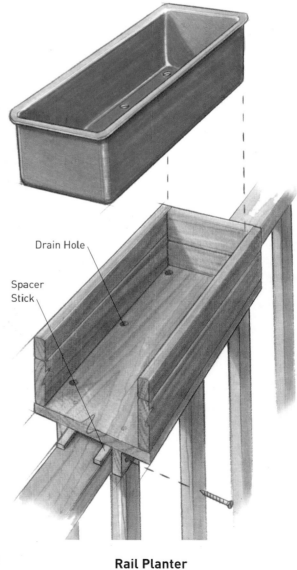

Rail Planter

Through the Deck

A through-the-deck garden bed is an ideal way to integrate your deck with the surrounding yard. On a small deck, it may seem like a waste of precious space, but it is a real time-saver when compared to using on-deck planters to accomplish similar results. That's because the soil in planters—even large ones—will get bone dry if you forget to add water or are away on vacation any length of time. The ground will dry out, too, but not nearly as fast—especially if you've added plenty of organic matter to the soil and covered it with mulch. If you live in a zone subject to freezes, an in-ground bed doesn't need to be emptied and stowed in the shed or basement the way ceramic pots (and even plastic ceramic look-alikes) do. The one drawback to a through-the-deck garden bed is that it is a potential tripping hazard. Encircle it with benches, planters, or a rope guard to prevent visitors from stepping backward into the opening. Light the area well at night.

1

2

③

④

Building Around Trees

Incorporating existing trees in your deck plan can create an exciting look. Besides, who likes to cut down healthy trees? Keep in mind, however, that accommodating a tree through your decking entails some extra framing and several precautions. The joist (or joists) that must be cut for the tree hole must be supported with a header so that adjacent joists will carry the load. (See "Framing for a Tree," page 200.) You cannot simply leave the cut joist unsupported. If the tree is mature and your deck is less than a few feet high, you can probably get away with a 2- or 3-inch gap between the hole and tree. For a younger tree that will continue to grow, allow a bigger gap to accommodate growth, or plan to enlarge the hole later. Allow for a larger gap around a young tree that passes through a raised deck, as well. The tree may need to sway slightly in a storm and you don't want it to damage itself or your deck.

1 Decks can be barren places without plants, and planters alone may not do the trick. Consider through-the-deck beds for larger plant masses and less watering.

2 Deck and landscape come together at this redwood-clad retaining wall.

3 It's a shame to cut down a healthy tree. Build around trees when possible, taking care not to excessively damage roots during excavation for deck and house footings.

4 This through-deck tree provides much-needed shade and helps reduce the deck's enormous scale.

Framing for a Tree

Framing to accommodate a tree may involve doubling up adjacent joists and installing headers to carry the joists you must cut—none of which is difficult. Scribe and cut deck boards to the shape of the tree prior to installing them.

Doubled Header

Doubled Joist

Right This large New England deck incorporates several trees, maintaining the rustic charm of the house. If necessary, holes for the trees can be enlarged with a heavy-duty saber saw as the girth of the trees expands.

①

What to Plant

For ground-level decks, plant choices are nearly unlimited. Perennials do the best job of filling in large areas. With the right amount of sun and fertile soil, they're great performers year after year. Once established, you'll be able to divide them and use them elsewhere in your yard.

Annuals are best in planters and often offer perpetual color all season long. They're not big feeders but generally prefer plenty of sun—typically six to eight hours a day. Sweet potato vine, heliotrope, and cascading varieties of petunias, lantana, verbena, and ivy geraniums are popular, but there are many others from which to choose. You will, of course, have to replant them every year.

For raised decks, consider flowering vines, shrubs, and trees. Flowering vines soften deck edges and offer something new and different to look at every day. They also give your deck a lush, secluded feeling while reducing glare and heat from the sun. Morning glories, clematis, wisteria, climbing roses, and jasmine are good choices. Allow them

1 A hybrid honeysuckle vine, such as the one shown here, blooms for long periods and is a great way to soften up the edges of a deck.

2 Morning glories, which are fast climbers and prolific bloomers, are wonderful deck or trellis companions.

3 A small deck built in the middle of a garden is a great place from which to enjoy your horticultural endeavors.

to climb on balustrades, trellises, pergolas, or arbors.

Shrubs and trees that have good volume or mass also look nice around a raised deck. Look for species with a horizontal growth habit to complement your deck without dominating it. Popular shrubs include flowering quince, butterfly bush, oakleaf hydrangea, and dwarf viburnum, to mention just a few. Small trees (under 25 feet) that grow about as wide as they are tall include Chinese dogwood, Japanese maple, redbud, cornelian cherry, Japanese white pine, and star magnolia. Consult with your local garden center for species that are best suited to your growing zone.

Smart Tip **Where to Plant**

In order to get the most enjoyment possible from garden beds, make them deep enough to be seen while seated on your deck. If you plant them too close to the deck perimeter, they will be hidden by the deck structure, especially with decks that are several feet off the ground.

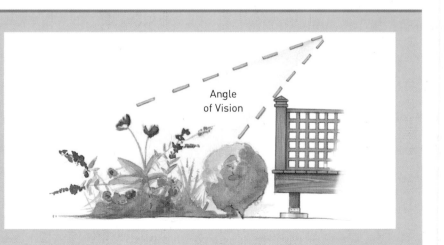

Angle of Vision

Choose Well-Behaved Plants

Avoid planting messy plants, such as berry bushes, near the deck. Also steer clear of sappy trees (sap draws aphids, and aphids attract ants). Fast-growing vines, such as wisteria, may become a nuisance as well. You'll have to trim some of the newer hybrids several times a year to keep them from jumping trellis or balustrade and entwining themselves around your patio furniture. On the other hand, the more you trim vines like wisteria, the more blossoms you'll get throughout the season. Afraid of bees? Avoid attractants such as jasmine and roses. Some well-behaved, low-maintenance choices include ornamental grasses, lavender, ferns, and evergreens (coniferous or broadleaf). Aside from being neat, evergreens provide a mass of green all year long and don't drop much debris in the way of leaves, seeds, and twigs.

1 Hydrangea, in many of its woody-stemmed varieties, is one of the most well-behaved flowering shrubs. Its blooms last from the middle of the summer through the fall; it needs very little maintenance; and it provides bountiful cuttings for drying and winter display.

2 English lavender, a no-fuss, no-muss perennial, is a good border plant for decks. Plant up front in a row of large shrubs intended for privacy or screening. Plant mid-depth in a cottage garden extending from your deck, as shown here.

1

Part 3

Gallery of Great Decks

Chapter 10

Ground-Level Decks

Ground-level decks have a lot going for them. For starters, they are easier to design than raised decks. They look good with nearly any style home and blend easily with the yard and gardens. They are also easier to build. Balustrades and stairs, two labor-intensive deck elements, are often unnecessary or are minimized. Fewer elements mean lower cost per square foot and less maintenance as well. Adding features, such as garden beds and fire pits, is also easier.

Ground-level decks also use yard space more efficiently than raised decks. The average 2-foot-high ground-level deck needs about 20 square feet of yard space for two stairs, while a deck that's raised 10 feet would need several times that for only one stairway—space that could be used for gardening and other activities. And ground-level decks are less likely to interfere with views from the house because guardrails, if there are any, are usually below window height. Low-level decks are generally safer than raised decks. Children can't mistake them for jungle gyms, and

adults, if they do step off the edge, have a shorter fall.

Ground-level decks, however, are not without their negative aspects. The biggest one is that the view from the deck is likely to be constrained. Ground-level decks often involve step-downs from the house or level changes on the deck itself, either of which can create tripping hazards. On the following pages, you'll find examples of ground-level decks.

Ground-level decks, like the waterfront one shown here, are easier to make feel at one with nature than other deck types.

Above Platform decks, such as this one, are literally at ground level. They're usually built on sleepers (pressure-treated 4x4s or 4x6s) that are set level on footings and a bed of gravel or sand. Platform decks are necessary when you have a door that is near grade. Detached decks, such as the one shown on page 234, are often built on grade as well.

Smart Tip **Hide the Framing**

The piers and beams that support most decks are not particularly interesting to look at. Many people go to considerable expense to hide them with skirting made of wood or composite slats or with lattice made of wood or vinyl. Eliminate the need for lattice skirting around your low-lying deck by keeping the deck low and using plants to hide the underpinnings. For decks that are several feet off the ground, plantings may not do the job until they mature. You may still be able to hide unsightly framing by locating piers 2 or 3 feet in from the deck perimeter and cantilevering joists and decking. (See illustration.) Note: If you do opt for this solution, installing skirting panels later will be somewhat more difficult because you will have no posts upon which to attach them.

Top right With this 30-in.-high contemporary deck, posts and beams were recessed and the decking was cantilevered for the last couple of feet. This makes the deck appear to be floating and echoes the deep eaves of the house.

Note: This detail works best on decks that are less than 3 ft. high.

Angle of Vision

1 Ground-level decks are often the best solution for "completing" a home's floor plan.

2 This redwood decking was treated with a clear sealer and with a toner, or semitransparent stain, to highlight the pattern.

3 The construction-heart-grade decking has small knots and other slight imperfections and is resistant to decay and insects.

4 A deck needn't be complex or large to be beautiful and serviceable, as this simple ground-level design proves.

Chapter 11

Raised Decks

Raised decks, whether they are only a few feet off the ground or 20 feet in the air, can open up dramatic views of your yard and beyond. They are ideal for extending the main level of homes built on sloping lots, where ground-level decks would be of limited use. They can also be used to connect second-story rooms in new and unusual ways.

Because of its prominence, a well-designed raised deck can help unify a disjointed house facade or add interest to a boring one. For homes built on rough terrain, raised decks often *become* the backyard.

Unlike ground-level decks, the space below a raised deck has lots of possible uses. As long as you install a drainage system to shed rain, you can use it for storing recreational and outdoor power equipment, as a workshop, or as an area for potting plants. You can also build a lower-level patio or deck. Tucked away from sun, wind, and rain, such a living space is ideal for an outdoor kitchen and dining area, or for a spa.

The negatives for raised decks are that they are more difficult to design and build. Complex construction translates into extra cost. Safety is a bigger concern, too, especially around stairs and guardrails. Finally, raised decks, especially high ones, are often great when you're standing on them but ungainly when viewed from the yard. Professional design help is highly recommended when embarking on such a project.

This chapter contains several outstanding examples of raised decks that manage to accentuate the positives and downplay the negatives. They include examples of how to use the space you create below the deck.

Large raised decks, such as this one, blend best when large posts or columns are used to support them.

Smart Tip **Keep It Neat below the Deck**

If you plan to use the space under an elevated deck for general storage—or simply if it will be open to view—keep it looking neat by installing a weed barrier under a layer of chipped stone or gravel. (See illustration.) Even if you're going to screen off the area under your deck, this is a good idea. You'll be amazed at how little light some weeds can live on. Stone yards offer a wide variety of gravel sizes and color. Pea gravel is best. Install a border of pressure-treated wood, brick, or stone blocks to keep the gravel from scattering. You may, of course, prefer to install a patio area under your upper-level deck.

Use a 3 oz. (minimum) woven polypropylene weed barrier that's needle-punched to allow rainwater to pass through.

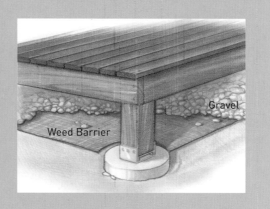

Weed Barrier

Gravel

1 Raised decks, such as this one, can transform a small second floor to an expansive outdoor recreation area.

2 This deck wraps around two sides of the second floor, allowing plenty of space for sunbathing and entertaining.

3 The spa is trimmed with the same slatted screening as the spa house.

4 The spa receives just enough sunlight, shares the deck's gorgeous views, and is well ventilated.

❹

Under-Deck Drainage Systems

If you're spending the time and money to build a second-level deck, invest a bit more in an under-deck drainage system and double your viable living space. Whether scratch-built with corrugated fiberglass panels or one of several commercially available roof membranes, it will keep the space below your deck dry.

Most under-deck drainage systems consist of rounded or V-shaped channels that are inserted between deck joists. They collect the rainwater that seeps between the deck boards and direct it to a center or side gutter. From there, it runs to one or more leaders (downspouts). The better sys-

tems are made of vinyl or aluminum and allow air to circulate beneath the deck boards, lessening the chance of rot. Be sure the components are sturdy enough to hold up should collected water freeze during the colder months. If you don't like the look of the system, much of it can be covered with something more decorative, such as cedar or bead-board. Allow for access to the gutter, however, as it may need to be cleaned out from time to time. With a dry area below, you open up many possibilities, including the installation of a ceiling fan, lighting, a spa, outdoor kitchen amenities, and the use of comfortable "indoor" types of furnishings that would otherwise be ruined by the weather.

1 Copper-toned gutters and a cedar ceiling hide the under-deck drainage system, creating a more finished appearance.

2 The patio below this upper-story deck stays dry during all but the most driving rainstorms.

3 The patio area is dry enough to add lights and a ceiling fan.

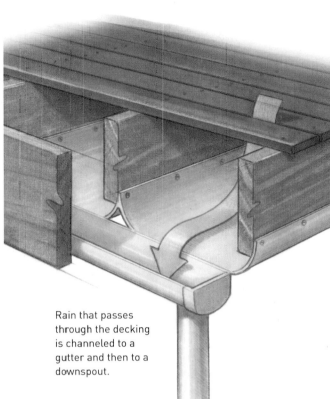

Rain that passes through the decking is channeled to a gutter and then to a downspout.

2

3

Chapter 12

Multilevel Decks

Multilevel decks are the best way to accommodate multiple activity areas, with each getting its own "room." The level changes act a bit like walls. With this approach, your dining area, spa, and kiddy pool all have their own space. Multilevel decks are also a good way to make the most of a sloping yard. Design the various levels so they hug the grade. In this way, even a large deck will seem smaller and not be so intrusive upon the landscape.

Varying levels are a good way to break up the mass of a large deck, so multilevel decks are sometimes better at blending with the architecture of a house. If the levels are separated by several feet or more, they can create the sort of intrigue that designers often strive for. At each level, new and surprising views open up. Level changes can also be used to seamlessly fit various deck fixtures into your plan. By installing a portable spa or grill counter against the "rise" of a level change, for example, you can create the illusion that it's a built-in.

On the other hand, multilevel decks have a tendency to become complicated—and often obscure the lines of the house with a confusion of stairs, balustrades, and irregularly-shaped platforms. Because of their complexity, it's wise to hire a designer or architect to help you with the plans. Multilevel decks can also be quite complicated to build, so you may want to start interviewing contractors as well. And remember: complexity translates into higher costs.

This multilevel deck is full of good ideas, including a spa, screened-in gazebo, food-prep counters, and under-deck storage.

1 When approaching this deck from the yard, one is greeted by planters and comfortable benches.

2 The architect who designed this deck used stonework, planters, and horizontal skirting to help "ground" the deck visually.

3 The trellis was placed to provide privacy during the winter, when trees are bare and the neighbors have a view of the spa.

4 A triangular cabinet with a granite countertop separates the cooking area from the dining area.

5 Below deck is storage for lawn equipment (page 173) and this potting shed.

④

Smart Tip **Hiring a Designer**

Before hiring any designer, be clear about what you want. Otherwise, you'll spend a lot of time and money to find out. The more work you do creating rough drawings or software-assisted drawings, the more efficient the design process will be. You will find many design sources for decks, including builders who also claim to be designers, manufacturers hoping to sell products, designers who work for firms that specialize in decks, and home centers that offer customizable modular deck systems. Licensed architects and designers with a strong architectural background are probably the most creative of the bunch, but their clever ideas can often add to the cost of the project unnecessarily. On the other hand, they will save you from making fundamental design errors and reduce misunderstanding with your builder. Your project is more likely to be successful with one than without.

⑤

1 Multilevel decks don't have to fill the yard. This one is compact, containing a spa and dining and lounging areas. Large wood-framed columns echo the house's simple, boxy shape.

2 The lower-level spa, trimmed using the same detail as the columns, is well away from the dining area but not shut off from views of the yard.

3 Redwood decking, benches, and tables are complemented by guardrails and column caps painted bright red. When the climbing plants on the awning-like trellis grow in, they will provide shade.

4 A triangular bumpout moves an activity area out of the traffic lane.

5 This three-level deck defines the look of this contemporary home. Glass panels open the view to the marshes.

6 Wood-slatted guardrails create privacy where it is needed the most.

7 Stairs on this multilevel deck lead from the mezzanine to this cozy rooftop hideaway.

Chapter 13

Specialty Decks

Many specialty decks are more or less opportunistic home improvement projects. They take advantage of a home's existing architectural features (and sometimes its foibles) and, with careful planning, turn it into something valuable.

Have a wasted, secluded space behind a garage that sees the sun rise? Build a small platform deck where you can read the morning newspaper and sip your coffee. Have a bedroom with a great view but a small window? Consider a balcony. Have an isolated spot in your backyard surrounded by gardens? Float the idea of a detached deck. Have a flat roof almost anywhere? Top it off with a roof deck.

Some specialty decks, however, solve architectural problems. An entry deck can convert a hidden doorway to a grand entrance—or at least one that visitors can easily spot. A pool or spa deck can vastly improve your poolside experience. It's much nicer than stone or tile if you want to spread out a towel and lie down. Wraparound decks run around corners and can link otherwise hard-to-

reach areas of the home, such as a kitchen and screened porch or kitchen and family room that's separated by a dining room. Wraparound or winding decks, used as walkways, are especially useful when your yard is too rough or steep to traverse.

Specialty decks—and decks in general—are a testament to the versatility of wood construction. It's light, fast, and inexpensive, and if designed well, can be quite elegant. Executing many of the examples shown in this chapter in stone would be unthinkable—or cost prohibitive. Combined with other materials, such as metals, glass, and plastics, today's decks offer more design options than ever before.

Decks can serve special purposes. This beautiful redwood deck provides comfortable places to sit at poolside.

1. Wraparound decks often serve as entry decks. This one helps give the front door more prominence.

2. Lighting, a key to the success of this deck, begins with an Arts and Crafts-style lantern.

3. The portion of the deck near the stone chimney is large enough to serve as an outdoor dining area.

4. Secondary stairs lead to the gardens and walking paths.

3

4

Smart Tip **Hiring a Contractor**

If you're planning to hire a contractor, he will help you work up a budget for your deck project. Just be sure to hire one that's reputable. Look for one that has been in business for at least a few years and has experience installing the type of deck in which you are interested. Request references, and check that his company's workman's compensation and liability insurance are up to date. If the contractor won't be doing the actual work, find out who will be (an employee or subcontractor, for example).

Ask for a contract that, in addition to total cost, specifies the grade of materials to be used, start and completion dates, cleanup standards at the end of each workday, and how change orders will be handled. (Change orders occur when you change your mind about some aspect of the job midstream.) In addition, discuss how the job will be handled. For example, who will replace and finish siding that is damaged during the installation of the ledger or a patio door? Who is responsible for disposing of old building materials and waste? Will the contractor supply portable facilities for his crew, or will he want access to your bathroom? It's best to meet with several contractors before signing a contract with the one who, all things considered, you think will do the best job for a reasonable amount of money.

❶

❷

1 This modern-style
home has an un-
derstated entrance
that's enhanced by
a small entry
deck. A wood
walkway leads to
the back of the
house.

2 From the entry,
the walkway
shown in photo 1
traverses the rear
elevation, well
above the uneven
terrain below, and
leads to the main
deck.

3 The main deck,
built of western
red cedar, has
ample room for
entertaining.

1 This multifamily home—like many of the homes built in the early part of the last century—was an excellent candidate for a balcony deck.

2 The deck, which was built over the second-story porch, provides tree-top views of the neighborhood without detracting from the design of the house.

3 Guardrails were constructed over the old roof to save space.

4 The decking and joists sit on a rubber roofing membrane. They can be lifted off if repairs to the roof are necessary.

5

6

5 The entrance to this rooftop deck is through the attic, but the views are worth the climb.

6 Balcony and rooftop decks can, of course, be added to more contemporary houses, as shown here.

Chapter 13 Specialty Decks

1 Detached decks are typically built on pressure-treated timbers set on top of a bed of gravel or sand for drainage. This creative example features a bridge over an ornamental streambed, which is a perfect foil for a shady rock garden.

2 The "at one with nature" effect is completed by putting in an ornamental pool with recirculating water for both sound and aeration. Low-voltage lighting allows the pool to be seen at night.

3 The deck connects to the front yard via a wood path.

4 Although detached, the deck is within earshot of the home's main deck, which sports a sizable garden shed below.

❷

❸

❹

235

❶

Smart Tip **Pool Surrounds**

Most backyard pools are of the above-ground variety. They're relatively inexpensive and easy to install. The big drawback is that you have to get into them from the ground, which usually involves climbing a slippery, flimsy plastic ladder. Deck surrounds are a good solution. They improve pool safety and usually enhance the look of a pool, as well.

❷

3

4

1 Composite decking is ideal around pools. It can be cut around intricate shapes, thereby eliminating toe-stubbing gaps, and it will not splinter.

2 The deck makes the adjacent aboveground pool more convenient and safer to use.

3 This pool deck was built by a homeowner using a floating deck system, which eliminated the need for footings.

4 Specially-cast concrete blocks hold the posts in position. Diagonal bracing keeps the assembly stable and distributes the weight evenly.

237

①

②

③

④

5

1 An in-ground pool (at right, out of view) benefits from this three-piece deck.

2 Both the deck mentioned above and the privacy fencing were constructed of redwood.

3 The cleverly-designed deck platforms look almost as if they're floating.

4 The deck is just wide enough for dining and lounging.

5 Wood decking works well in combination with stone or terra-cotta tiling, as shown here.

Distinctive Deck Designs

Raised Deck with Sweeping Overlook

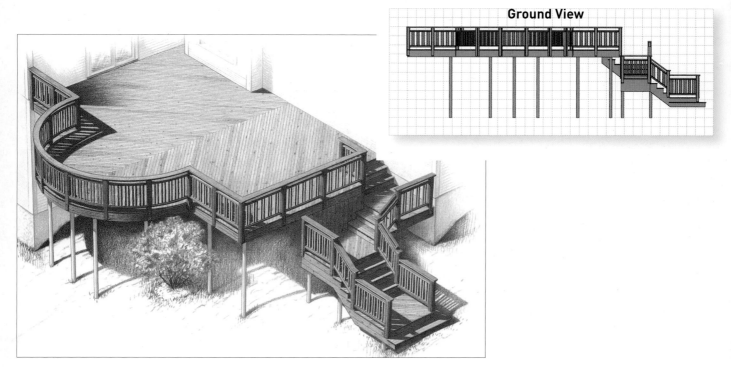

Ground View

Raised Deck with Sweeping Overlook, Plan View

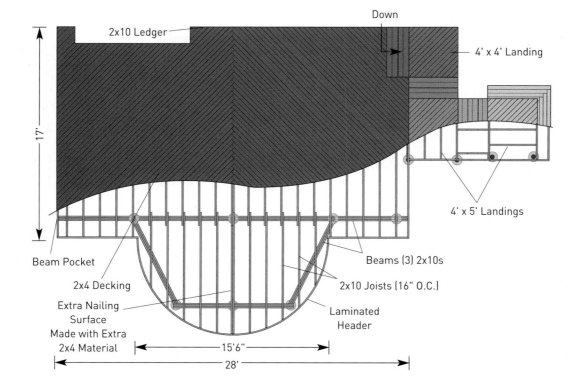

Down

2x10 Ledger

4' x 4' Landing

4' x 5' Landings

17'

Beam Pocket

2x4 Decking

Extra Nailing
Surface
Made with Extra
2x4 Material

15'6"

28'

Beams (3) 2x10s

2x10 Joists (16" O.C.)

Laminated
Header

Front Porch/Deck for a Corner Lot

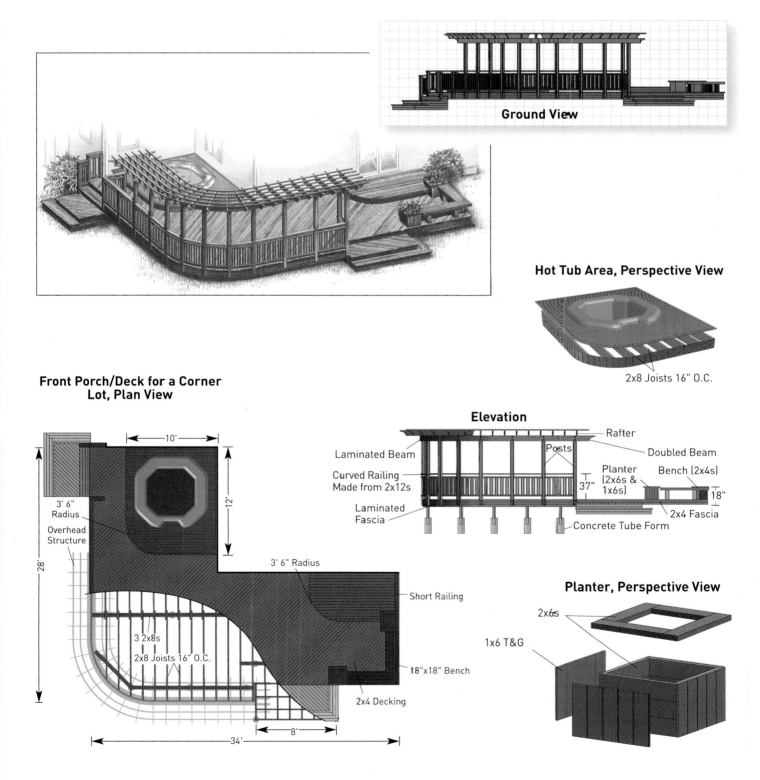

Ground View

Hot Tub Area, Perspective View

2x8 Joists 16" O.C.

Front Porch/Deck for a Corner Lot, Plan View

10'

12'

3' 6"
Radius

Overhead
Structure

28'

3' 6" Radius

Short Railing

3 2x8s

2x8 Joists 16" O.C.

18"x18" Bench

2x4 Decking

8'

34'

Elevation

Rafter

Laminated Beam

Posts

Doubled Beam

Curved Railing
Made from 2x12s

Planter
(2x6s &
1x6s)

Bench (2x4s)

37"

18"

Laminated
Fascia

2x4 Fascia

Concrete Tube Form

Planter, Perspective View

2x6s

1x6 T&G

BEST-SELLING DECK PLANS

How Many Plans Should You Order?

Minimum 5-Set Package. If you are in the bidding process, you may want to order only five sets for the bidding round and reorder additional sets as needed.

1-Set Study Package. The 1-set package allows you to review your deck plan in detail. The plan will be marked as a study print, and it is illegal to build a deck from a study print alone. It is a violation of copyright law to reproduce a blueprint without permission.

Buying Additional Sets

If you require additional copies of blueprints for your deck, you can order additional sets within 60 days of the original order date at a reduced price. The cost is $45.00 for each additional set. Contact customer service for details.

Reproducible Masters

If you plan to make minor changes to one of our deck plans, you can purchase reproducible masters. Printed on vellum paper, an erasable paper that you can reproduce in a copying machine, reproducible masters allow an architect, designer, or builder to alter our plans to give you a customized deck design. This package also allows you to print as many copies of the modified plans as you need for construction.

CAD Files

CAD files are the complete set of deck plans in an electronic file format. Choose this option if there are multiple changes you wish made to the deck plans and you have a local design professional able to make the changes. Not available for all plans. Please contact our order department or visit our Web site to check the availability of CAD files for your plan.

Mirror-Reverse Sets/Right-Reading Reverse

Plans can be printed in mirror-reverse—we can "flip" plans to create a mirror image of the design. This is useful when the deck would fit your site or personal preferences if all the features were on the opposite side than shown. As the image is reversed, the lettering and dimensions will also be reversed, meaning they will read backwards. Therefore, when ordering mirror-reverse drawings, you must order at least one set of right-reading plans. A $50.00 fee per plan order will be charged for mirror-reverse (regardless of the number of mirror-reverse sets ordered). Some plans are available in right-reading reverse, this feature will show the plan in reverse, but the writing on the plan will be readable. A $150.00 fee per plan order will be charged for right-reading reverse (regardless of the number of right-reading reverse sets ordered). Please contact our order department or visit our website to check the availibility of this feature for your chosen plan.

Materials List

The Materials List provides you an invaluable resource in planning and estimating the cost of your deck. Each Materials List outlines the quantity, dimensions, and type of materials needed to build your deck. You will get faster, more-accurate bids from your contractors and building suppliers—and avoid paying for unused materials. A Materials List is included with each plan order.

Order Toll Free by Phone
1-800-523-6789
By Fax: 201-760-2431

Regular office hours are
8:30AM–7:30PM ET, Mon–Fri

Orders received 3PM ET, will be processed
and shipped within two business days.

Order Online
www.ultimateplans.com

Mail Your Order
Creative Homeowner
Attn: Home Plans
24 Park Way
Upper Saddle River, NJ 07458

Canadian Customers
Order Toll Free 1-800-393-1883

Mail Your Order (Canada)
Creative Homeowner Canada
Attn: Home Plans
113-437 Martin St., Ste. 215
Penticton, BC V2A 5L1

Before You Order

Our Exchange Policy

Blueprints are nonrefundable. However, should you find that the plan you have purchased does not fit your needs, you may exchange that plan for another plan in our collection within 60 days from the date of your original order. The entire content of your original order must be returned before an exchange will be processed. You will be charged a processing fee of 20% of the amount of the original order, the cost difference between the new plan set and the original plan set (if applicable), and all related shipping costs for the new plans. Contact our order department for more information. Please note: reproducible masters may only be exchanged if the package is unopened, and CAD files are nonrefundable and cannot be exchanged.

Building Codes and Requirements

At the time of creation, our plans meet the bulding code requirements published by the Building Officials and Code Administrators International, the Southern Building Code Congress International, the International Conference of Building Officials, or the Council of American Building Officials. Because building codes vary from area to area, some drawing modifications and/or the assistance of a professional designer or architect may be necessary to comply with your local codes or to accommodate specific building site conditions. We strongly advise you to consult with your local building official for information regarding codes governing your area.

Blueprint Price Schedule

Price Code	1 Set	5 Sets	Reproducible Masters	CAD	Materials List
AA	$60	$85	$125	$425	Included
BB	$85	$105	$150	$450	Included
CC	$110	$135	$175	$475	Included
DD	$135	$155	$200	$500	Included
EE	$150	$180	$230	$530	Included
FF	$190	$220	$270	$570	Included

Note: all prices subject to change

Shipping & Handling

Shipping & Handling	1-4 Sets	5-7 Sets	8+ Sets or Reproducibles	CAD
US Regular (7–10 business days)	$18	$20	$25	$25
US Priority (3–5 business days)	$25	$30	$35	$35
US Express (1–2 business days)	$40	$45	$50	$50
Worldwide Express (3–5 business days)	$100	$100	$100	$100

Note: all delivery times are from date the blueprint package is shipped (typically within 1-2 days of placing order).

Order Form
Please send me the following:

Plan Number: _____ **Price Code:** _____

Basic Blueprint Package	Cost
❏ CAD File	
❏ Reproducible Masters	$_____
❏ 5-Set Plan Package	$_____
❏ 1-Set Study Package	$_____
❏ Additional plan sets: __ sets at $45.00 per set	$_____
❏ Print in mirror-reverse: $50.00 per order *Please call all our order department or visit our website for availibility	$_____
❏ Print in right-reading reverse: $150.00 per order *Please call all our order department or visit our website for availibility	$_____
Shipping (see chart above)	$_____
SUBTOTAL	$_____
Sales Tax (NJ residents only, add 7%)	$_____
TOTAL	$_____

SOURCE CODE **CA604**

Order Toll Free: 1-800-523-6789 By Fax: 201-760-2431
Creative Homeowner
24 Park Way
Upper Saddle River, NJ 07458

Name _____
(Please print or type)

Street _____
(Please do not use a P.O. Box)

City _____ State _____

Country _____ Zip _____

Daytime telephone ( ) _____

Fax ( ) _____
(Required for reproducible orders)

E-Mail _____

Payment ❏ Bank check or money order. No personal checks.
(Make checks payable to Creative Homeowner)

❏ VISA   ❏ MasterCard   ❏ AMERICAN EXPRESS Cards   ❏ DISCOVER

Credit card number _____

Expiration date (mm/yy) _____

Signature _____

Please check the appropriate box:
❏ Licensed builder/contractor   ❏ Homeowner   ❏ Renter

Deck with Gazebo

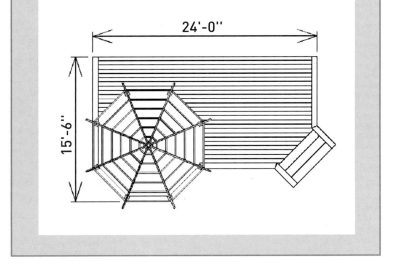

24'-0"

15'-6"

CH # 321084 PRICE CODE: **AA**

- Dimensions: 24'-0" × 15'-6"
- Height, floor to peak: 12'-2"
- Perfect for outdoor entertaining
- Gazebo adds unique flair to this deck
- Complete list of materials
- Step-by-step instructions

Low Patio Decks

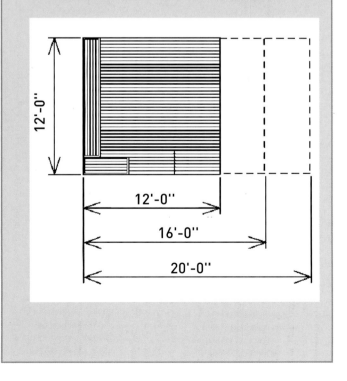

CH # 321086

- Three popular sizes: 12' × 12', 16' × 12', or 20' × 12'
- Built-in seating
- Perfect for entertaining
- Complete list of materials
- Step-by-step instructions

247

Raised Patio Decks

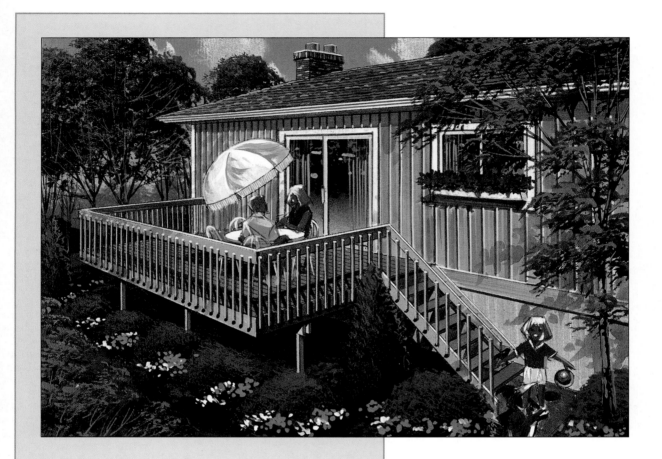

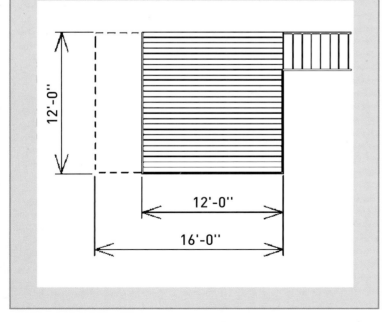

CH # 321087   PRICE CODE: **AA**

- Two popular sizes: 12' × 12', 16' × 12'
- Both decks can be constructed at any height
- Can be built to fit any lot situation
- Complete list of materials
- Step-by-step instructions

Pool Deck

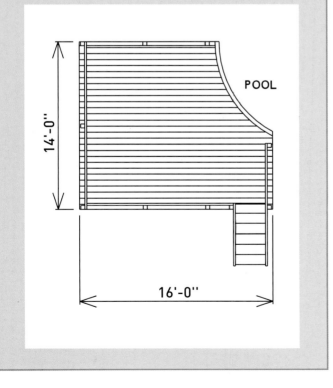

CH # 321088

- Dimensions: 16' W × 14' D
- Can be built to fit any size pool
- Simple but sturdy design with built-in gate
- Makes cleaning and maintaining pool a breeze
- Complete list of materials
- Step-by-step instructions

Two-Level Deck

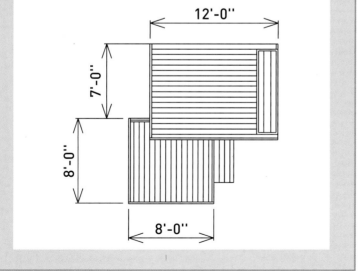

12'-0"

7'-0"

8'-0"

8'-0"

CH # 321089   PRICE CODE: **AA**

- Overall size: 14' × 15'
    - Lower deck: 8' × 8'
    - Upper deck: 12' × 9'
- Unique, attractive design features two-level deck and bench
- Adds great value to your home
- Complete list of materials
- Step-by-step instructions

Shaded Deck

CH # 321090   PRICE CODE: **AA**

- Dimensions: 16' W × 10' D × 9'-6" H
- Deck design has a sun-screen covering
- Enhance the outdoors with this shaded deck
- Complete list of materials
- Step-by-step instructions

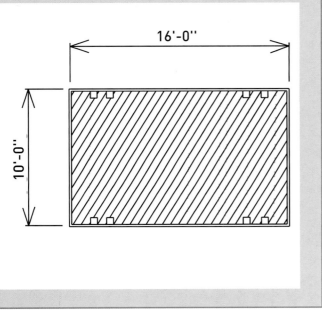

16'-0"

10'-0"

Two-Level Garden Deck

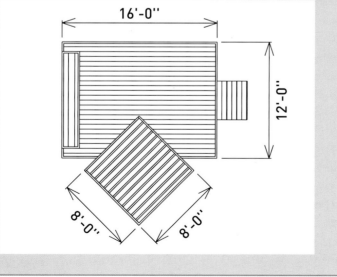

16'-0"

12'-0"

8'-0"

8'-0"

CH # 321091 PRICE CODE: AA

- Overall size: 16' × 19'
  - Lower deck: 16' × 12'
  - Upper deck: 8' × 8'
- Unique design features decorative plant display area or sundeck
- Built-in seating
- Can be freestanding or attached
- Complete list of materials
- Step-by-step instructions

High Low Deck

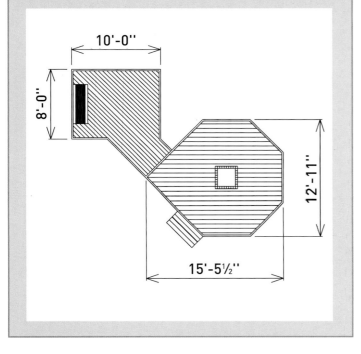

CH # 321092

PRICE CODE: **AA**

- Lower deck: 15' × 13'
- Upper deck: 10' × 8'
- Designed as an add-on to an existing deck or as a complete unit
- Benches can be arranged as needed
- Features a unique conversation area or optional fire pit
- Complete list of materials
- Step-by-step instructions

Easy Decks

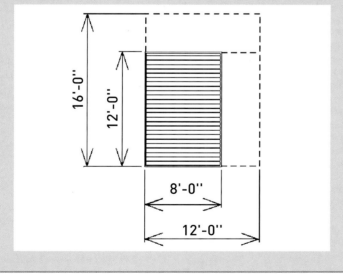

CH # 321093   PRICE CODE: **AA**

- Three great sizes: 8' × 12', 12' × 12', or 12' × 16'
- Low cost construction
- Can be built with standard lumber
- Adaptable to all grades
- Complete list of materials
- Step-by-step instructions

Split-Level Deck

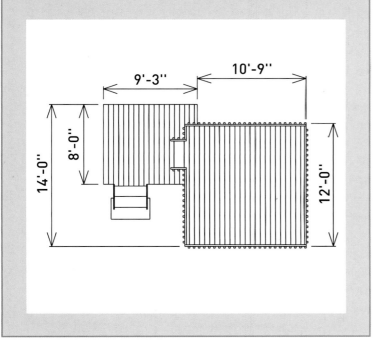

CH # 321094 PRICE CODE: AA

- Overall size: 20' × 14'
  - Lower deck: 9' × 8'
  - Upper deck: 12' × 12'
- Can be built with standard lumber
- Adaptable to all grades
- Complete list of materials
- Step-by-step instructions

Two-Level Spa Deck

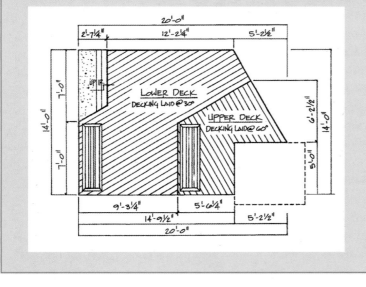

CH # 321095   PRICE CODE: **AA**

- Overall size: 20' × 14'
  - Lower deck: 14'-9'' × 14'
  - Upper deck: 10'-9'' × 11'-3''
- Designed for self-contained portable spas
- Freestanding or next to house
- Complete list of materials
- Step-by-step instructions

Two-Level Raised Deck

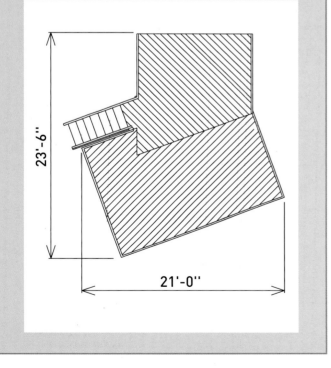

CH # 321096

- Overall size: 21' × 24'
  - Lower deck: 18' × 12'
  - Upper deck: 12' × 12'-9"
- Can be built at any height
- Adaptable to any lot situation
- Complete list of materials
- Step-by-step instructions

Hexagon Deck

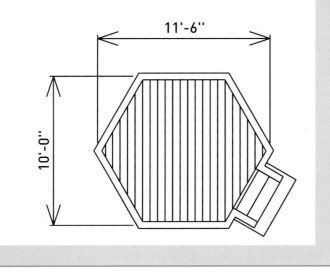

11'-6"

10'-0"

CH # 321097   PRICE CODE: **AA**

- Dimensions: 11'-6" W × 10' D
- Freestanding design
- Attractive deck with a choice of two railing styles
- Simple construction—easy to build
- Complete list of materials
- Step-by-step instructions

Deck with Sunken Dining Area

CH # 321098
PRICE CODE: **AA**

- Two popular sizes: 16' × 16', 18' × 18'
- Unique sunken area adds interest to this deck
- Perfect addition to enhance outdoor entertaining
- Complete list of materials
- Step-by-step instructions

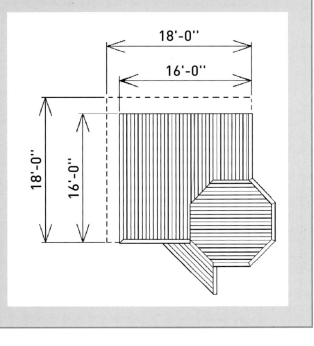

Bay Deck with Railing

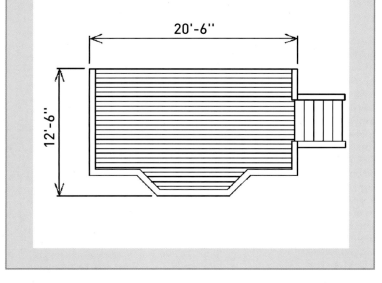

20'-6"

12'-6"

CH # 321099   PRICE CODE: **AA**

- Dimensions: 20'-6" W × 12'-6" D
- Adds beauty and value to your home
- Unique layout with built-in bay
- Complete list of materials
- Step-by-step instructions

Tiered Deck with Gazebo

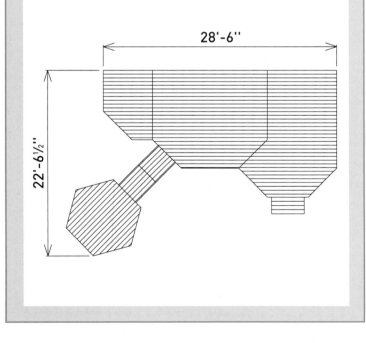

CH # 321100   PRICE CODE: **AA**

- Overall area: 28'-6'' W × 15'-6'' D

  (without gazebo)

  - Deck A: 9' W × 15'-6'' D

  - Deck B: 6'-6'' W × 8'-6'' D

  - Deck C: 14' W × 12' D

  - Gazebo D: 9'-6'' W × 8'-3'' D (sided)

- Walkway E: 3' W × 7' D

- Gazebo offers privacy and shade

- Build complete or add on later

- Complete list of materials

- Step-by-step instructions

Expandable Decks

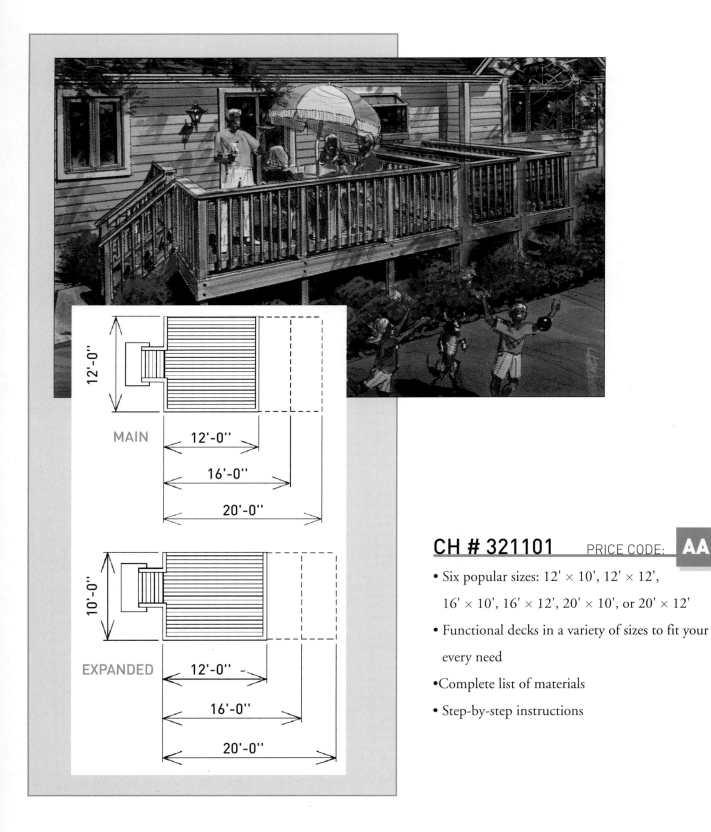

MAIN

12'-0"

12'-0"

16'-0"

20'-0"

EXPANDED

10'-0"

12'-0"

16'-0"

20'-0"

CH # 321101   PRICE CODE: **AA**

- Six popular sizes: 12' × 10', 12' × 12', 16' × 10', 16' × 12', 20' × 10', or 20' × 12'
- Functional decks in a variety of sizes to fit your every need
- Complete list of materials
- Step-by-step instructions

Ground-Level Decks

CH # 391228   PRICE CODE: **AA**

- Package Contains 12 Different Sizes:

  8' × 8', 8' × 10', 8' × 12',

  10' × 10', 10' × 12', 10' × 16',

  12' × 12', 12' × 16', 14' × 20',

  14' × 16', 16' × 16', or 16' × 20'

Easy-Build Decks

CH # 391229   PRICE CODE: **AA**

- Stair and railing plans included
- Package contains 8 different sizes:

  8' × 8', 8' × 10', 8' × 12',

  10' × 10', 10' × 12', 10' × 16',

  12' × 12', or 12' × 16'

Decks with Pergola

CH # 391230   PRICE CODE: **AA**

- Stair, railing and optional trellis plans
- Package contains 4 different sizes: 14' × 16', 16' × 16', 14' × 20', or 16' × 20'

Small Pool Deck

CH # 391231   PRICE CODE: **AA**

- Dimensions: 12' W × 12' D
- Stair and railing, optional privacy screen, gate and step to house plans included

Large Pool Deck

CH # 391232   PRICE CODE: **AA**

- Stairs, railing and trellis plans included
- Package contains three different sizes to fit around a 15', 18', or 24' wide pool (adaptable to any pool length)

Multilevel Deck

CH # 391233   PRICE CODE: **AA**

- Dimensions: 10' W × 14' D
- Stair and railing, optional privacy screen, gate and step to house plans included

Play Area Deck

CH # 391234   PRICE CODE: **AA**

- Stairs, railing and playground equipment plans included
- 14' × 14' upper deck adjustable to any height
- 8' × 12' lower deck

Double Decks

CH # 391235   PRICE CODE: **AA**

- 12' x 16' upper deck with additional step
- Three different sizes for the lower deck: 10' × 12', 12' × 14', or 14' × 16'

Deck with Planters

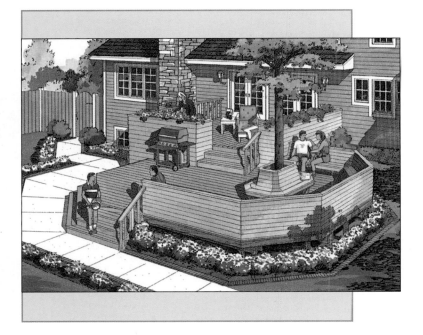

CH # 391236   PRICE CODE: **AA**

- Stairs, railing, planter and bench plans included

Wraparound Decks

CH # 391237   PRICE CODE: **AA**

- Build the stairs where you want them
- Stair and railing plans included
- Eight different sizes

Decks with Alcove

CH # 391238 PRICE CODE: **AA**

- Includes extra-wide railing and stair plans
- 8-sided 10' diameter raised picnic area
- Lower deck can be built in five sizes: 12' × 12', 12' × 16', 12' × 20', 14' × 16' or 14' × 20'

Pocket-Size Decks

CH # 391239 PRICE CODE: **AA**

- Stair, railing, planter and optional bench plans included
- Two different sizes for upper deck: 8' × 12' or 8' × 14'
- Four different sizes for lower deck: 8' × 12', 8' × 14', 10' × 12', or 10' × 14'

Gazebo Decks

CH # 391240   PRICE CODE: **AA**

- 10' diameter picnic deck and gazebo
- Two different main deck sizes

Distinctive Railing Design

CH # 391241   PRICE CODE: **AA**

- Optional diagonal decking
- Eight size options included

Step-Down Decks

CH # 391242 PRICE CODE: **AA**

- Four deck size combinations:

  Upper deck: 12' × 8' or 12' × 10'

  Lower deck: 18' × 12' or 20' × 12'

Basic Decks

CH # 391243 PRICE CODE: **AA**

- Instructional package provides general construction techniques and details on how to build decks
- Three different styles of construction: rectangular, octagonal, multilevel

Rectangular Decks

CH # 391244   PRICE CODE: **AA**

- Low maintenance decking and PVC railing components
- Eight sizes: 8' × 8', 8' × 12', 10' × 10', 10' × 12', 12' × 12', 12' × 18', 12' × 24', or 18' × 24'

Separate Activity Area

CH # 391245   PRICE CODE: **AA**

- Side door and stair plans included
- 4:12 pitch roof that attaches to side or roof of house
- Six sizes: 8' × 12', 10' × 12', 12' × 12', 8' × 16', 10' × 16', or 12' × 16'

Resource Guide

The following list of manufacturers and associations is meant to be a general guide to additional industry and product-related sources. It is not intended as a listing of products and manufacturers represented by the photographs in this book.

Alcoa Home Exteriors
201 Isabella St.
Pittsburgh, PA 15212-5858
800-962-6973
www.alcoa.com/alcoahomes
Manufactures aluminum and synthetic building materials, including deck products under the Oasis brand.

Alumatec Industries Inc.
529 Orange Ave.
Daytona, FL 32114
800-989-7245
www.alumatecindustries.com
Manufactures and installs a complete line of aluminum, stainless-steel, and brass railings.

Andersen Corporation
100 Fourth Ave. North
Bayport, MN 55003-1096
800-426-4261
www.andersenwindows.com
Offers a full line of patio doors and windows.

APA – The Engineered Wood Association
7011 South 19th St.
Tacoma, WA 98466
253-565-6600
www.apawood.org
A nonprofit trade association that produces a variety of engineered wood products.

AridDek
1604 Athens Hwy.
Gainesville, GA 30507
877-270-9387
www.ariddek.com
Manufactures aluminum decking and railings.

AZEK Trimboards
801 Corey St.
Moosic, PA 18507
877-275-2935
www.azek.com
Synthetic trim products, including balustrades, moldings, and lattice skirting.

Blue Rhino Corporation
104 Cambridge Plaza Dr.
Winston-Salem, NC 27104
800-762-1142
www.uniflame.com
Offers a full line of grills, heaters, and other outdoor appliances, plus a propane tank exchange program.

CableRail/Feeney Architectural Products
2603 Union St.
Oakland, CA 94607
800-888-2418
www.cablerail.com
Manufactures a line of standard and custom cable stainless-steel cable assemblies.

California Redwood Association
405 Enfrente Dr., Suite 200
Novato, CA 94949-7206
888-225-7339
www.calredwood.org
Offers technical information about the use of redwood for decks and other structures.

Cascades
404 Marie-Victorin Blvd.
Kingsey Falls, QC, Canada J0A 1B0
819-363-5100
www.cascades.com

A packaging product leader that also makes decking from recycled plastic under the Perma-deck brand.

Cecco Trading, Inc.
600 East Vienna Ave.
Milwaukee, WI 53212
414-445-8989
www.ironwoods.com
Supplies the Iron Wood brand of Ipe hardwood lumber. Check the Web site to locate a lumber yard near you.

Correct Building Products
8 Morin St.
Biddeford, ME 04005
877-332-5877
www.correctdeck.com
Maker of CorrectDeck, a composite decking material.

Deck Images
12590 127th St. South
Hastings, MN 55033
877-446-7397
www.deckimages.com
Manufactures powder-coated aluminum and glass railing systems for residential and commercial markets.

Deckmaster
205 Mason Cir.
Concord, CA 94520
800-869-1375
www.deckmaster.com
Makes bracket-style hidden deck fasteners.

Deckorators
50 Crestwood Executive Center, Suite 308
Crestwood, MO 63126
800-332-5724
www.deckorators.com

Manufactures a wide range of aluminum balustrades and glass railings in many colors and designs.

DekBrands
P.O. Box 14804
Minneapolis, MN 55414
800-664-2705
www.deckplans.com
Manufacturer of easy-to-do deck systems, including the award-winning Floating Foundation Deck System.

DESA
2701 Industrial Dr.
Bowling Green, KY 42101
866-672-6040
www.desatech.com
Maker of security lights with motion detectors and deck heaters, including umbrella stands with built-in heaters.

Dry-B-Lo
475 Tribble Gap Rd., Suite 305
Cumming, GA 30040
800-437-9256
www.dry-b-lo.com
Manufactures aluminum deck drainage systems that keep the space below decks dry.

EB-TY Hidden Deck-Fastening Systems
Blue Heron Enterprises, LLC
P.O. Box 5389
North Branch, NJ 08876
800-438-3289
www.ebty.com
Makes biscuit-style hidden deck fasteners.

Empyrean International, LLC
930 Main St.
Acton, MA 01720

800-727-3325

www.empyreanapf.com

Custom-designed homes that often feature decks. Brands include Deck House, Acorn, and The Dwell Homes by Empyrean.

EverGrain Composite Decking, a div. of TAMKO Building Products, Inc.

P.O. Box 1404

Joplin, MO 64802

800-253-1401

www.evergrain.com

Manufactures composite decking products with realistic, compression-molded graining patterns.

Forest Stewardship Council-U.S.

1155 30th St. NW, Suite 300

Washington, D.C. 20007

202-342-0413

www.fscus.org

A nonprofit organization devoted to encouraging the responsible management of the world's forests.

Gaco Western

P.O. Box 88698

Seattle, WA 98138

866-422-6489

www.gaco.com

Manufactures a high-quality acrylic polymer waterproof surface protection for plywood or plank decks.

Gale Pacific

P.O. Box 951509

Lake Mary, FL 32795-1509

800-560-4667

www.coolaroo.com

Manufactures a wide range of outdoor fabrics with various degrees of UV protection.

Grace Construction Products

62 Whittemore Ave.

Cambridge, MA 02140

800-354-5414

www.graceconstruction.com

www.graceathome.com

Offers self-adhering flashing for decks.

Hadco Lighting, a div. of Genlyte Group Inc.

100 Craftway

Littlestown, PA 17340

800-331-4185

www.hadcolighting.com

Offers a large variety of outdoor lighting designed for decks, including post, step, path, and area lights.

Hearth & Home Technologies

20802 Kensington Blvd.

Lakeville, MN 55044

888-669-4328

www.hearthnhome.com

Offers a complete line of gas, electric, and wood-burning heating products.

Highpoint Deck Lighting

P.O. Box 428

Black Hawk, CO 80422

888-582-5850

www.hpdlighting.com

Produces a full line of outdoor lighting, including railing lights, recessed step lights, hanging lanterns, wall sconces, and barbecue cook lights.

Hooks and Lattice

5671 Palmer Way, Suite K

Carlsbad, CA 92010

800-896-0978

www.hooksandlattice.com
Web site features all styles of window boxes designed for every application, including deck railings.

Jacuzzi
14525 Monte Vista Ave.
Chino, CA 91710
866-234-7727
www.jacuzzi.com
Manufactures a full line of hot tubs and deck spas.

LockDry
FSI Home Products Division
2700 Alabama Highway 69 South
Cullman, AL 35057
800-711-1785
www.lockdry.com
Patented aluminum deck and railing systems with built-in continuous gutters.

Marvin Windows and Doors
P.O. Box 100
Warroad, MN 56763
888-537-7828
www.marvin.com
Makers of a full line of windows and doors, including sliders and French doors.

NanaWall Systems, Inc.
707 Redwood Hwy.
Mill Valley, CA 94941
800-873-5673
www.nanawall.com
Manufactures folding wall systems of easy-to-open glass panels.

National Fenestration Rating Council (NFRC)
8484 Georgia Ave., Suite 320
Silver Spring, MD 20910
301-589-1776
www.nfrc.org
A nonprofit organization that administers the only uniform, independent rating and labeling system for the energy performance of patio doors and other products.

Pella Corporation
102 Main St.
Pella, IA 50219
800-374-4758
www.pella.com
Produces energy-efficient patio doors and windows.

Procell Decking Systems
11746 Foley Beach Express
Foley, AL 36535
251-943-2916
www.procelldeck.com
Manufactures synthetic decking from PVC that's stain- and scratch-resistant.

Progress Lighting
P.O. Box 5704
Spartanburg, SC 29304-5704
864-599-6000
www.progresslighting.com
Makes wall lanterns that have motion detectors built into the mounting plate or the lantern itself, as well as deck and landscape lights.

Punch! Software, LLC
7900 NW 100th St., Suite LL6
Kansas City, MO 64153
800-365-4832
www.punchsoftware.com
Software company specializing in home and landscaping design programs.

Royal Crown Limited
P.O. Box 360
Milford, IN 46542-0360
800-488-5245
www.royalcrownltd.com
Produces vinyl deck planks and railing products under
the Triple Crown Fence, Brock Deck Systems, Brock
Deck, and Deck Lok Systems brands.

Shade Sails LLC
7028 Greenleaf Ave., Suite K
Whittier, CA 90602
562-945-9952
www.shadesails.com
Imports tensioned, UV-treated fabric canopies.

ShadeScapes USA
39300 Back River Rd.
Paonia, CO 81428
866-997-4233
www.shadescapesusa.com
Manufactures side- and center-post shade umbrellas.

Southern Pine Council
2900 Indiana Ave.
Kenner, LA 70065-4605
504-443-4464
www.southernpine.com
A trade association that offers information on deck
building with treated lumber.

Starborn Industries, Inc.
27 Engelhard Ave.
Avenel, NJ 07001
800-596-7747
www.starbornindustries.com
Manufactures stainless-steel deck fastening systems,
including Headcote and DeckFast brand screws.

Summer Classics
P.O. Box 390
7000 Highway 25
Montevallo, AL 35115
205-987-3100
www.summerclassics.com
Manufactures deck and garden furnishings in wrought
aluminum, wrought iron and woven resin.

Summerwood Products
735 Progress Ave.
Toronto, ON, Canada M1H 2W7
866-519-4634
www.summerwood.com
Offers prefab customized kits for outdoor structures
such as gazebos, pool cabanas, and spa enclosures.

Sundance Spas
14525 Monte Vista Ave.
Chino, CA 91710
800-883-7727
www.sundancespas.com
The largest manufacturer of acrylic spas.

Sustainable Forestry Initiative
American Forest & Paper Association
1111 Nineteenth St. NW, Suite 800
Washington, D.C. 20036
www.aboutsfi.org
A comprehensive forestry management program devel-
oped by the American Forest & Paper Association.

TAMKO Building Products, Inc.
EverGrain Composite Decking
Elements Decking
220 West 4th St.
Joplin, MO 64801
800-641-4691

www.tamko.com

www.evergrain.com

www.elementsdecking.com

Manufactures composite decking products using compression molding for a real wood look. Visit the Web site for a photo gallery and distributors in your area.

Tiger Claw Inc.

400 Middle St., Suite J

Bristol, CT 06010-8405

800-928-4437

www.deckfastener.com

Manufactures products for the construction industry, including hidden deck fasteners.

TimberTech

894 Prairie Ave.

Wilmington, OH 45177

800-307-7780

www.timbertech.com

Manufacturers composite decking and railing systems, fascia boards, and specialty trim.

Timber Treatment Technologies

8700 Trail Lake Dr., Suite 101

Germantown, TN 38125

866-318-9432

www.timbersil.com

Developer of a new process for preserving wood. The formula, nontoxic and noncorrosive, is designed for both aboveground and in-ground applications.

Trex Company, Inc.

160 Exeter Dr.

Winchester, VA 22603

800-289-8739

www.trex.com

Specializes in composite decking materials.

Universal Forest Products, Inc.

2801 East Beltline Ave. NE

Grand Rapids, MI 49525

616-364-6161

www.ufpi.com

Manufactures and distributes wood and wood-alternative products for decking and railing systems. Also manufactures Veranda brand products for Home Depot.

Western Red Cedar Lumber Association (WRCLA)

1501-700 West Pender St.

Pender Place 1, Business Building

Vancouver, BC, Canada V6C 1G8

866-778-9096

www.realcedar.org

www.wrcla.org

www.cedar-deck.org

A nonprofit trade association representing quality producers of western red cedar in the U.S. and Canada. Its Web site explains how to select appropriate grades.

Weyerhaeuser Co.

P.O. Box 1237

Springdale, AR 72765

800-951-5117

www.choicedek.com

Offers ChoiceDek brand decking manufactured from a blend of low- and high-density polyethylene plastic and wood fibers. Also distributes CedarOne cedar decking.

Wolman Wood Care Products, a div. of Zinsser Co., Inc.

173 Belmont Dr.

Somerset, NJ 08875

800-556-7737

www.wolman.com

Makes products used to restore, beautify, and protect decks and other exterior wood structures.

Glossary

Accent lighting Lighting that highlights a surface or object to emphasize its character.

Arbor A freestanding wooden structure upon which vines are grown to create a shady retreat.

Awning A roof-like structure, often made of weather-resistant canvas or plastic, that's attached to an exterior wall to provide shelter.

Balusters The vertical pieces, generally made of 2x2s, that fill the spaces between rails and posts to create a guardrail.

Balustrade A guardrail, often used around the perimeter of a deck, consisting of balusters, posts, and top and bottom rails.

Beam The term for any large horizontal framing member.

Blind fasteners Clips, brackets, or biscuits used to fasten decking to joists in such a way as to be hidden from view. An alternative to top-driven nails and screws.

Building codes Municipal rules regulating safe building practices and procedures. Generally, the codes encompass structural, electrical, plumbing, and mechanical remodeling and new construction.

Building permit An authorization to build or renovate according to plans approved by the local building department. Generally, any job that includes a footing or foundation or that involves any structural work requires a permit.

Built-in Any element, such as a bench or planter, that is attached permanently to the deck.

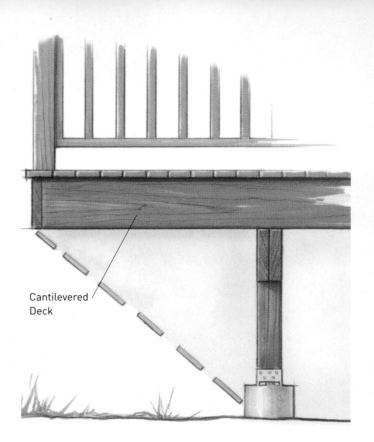

Cantilevered Deck

Cantilever Construction that extends horizontally beyond its support.

Clearance The amount of recommended space between two fixtures, such as between a grill and railing. Some clearances may be mandated by building codes.

Column A supporting pillar consisting of a base, a cylindrical shaft, and a capital.

Composite Building materials, including deck planking and railings, that are made by combining wood waste or fiber with plastics.

Cornice A horizontal molding that projects from the top of a wall to create a finished or decorative appearance.

Decay-resistant woods Woods, such as redwood and cedar, that are naturally resistant to rot.

Decking Boards fastened to joists to form the deck surface.

Eave The lower edge of a roof that overhangs a wall.

Exposure Contact with the sun's rays, wind, and in-clement weather.

Fascia Horizontal boards that cover the joint between the top of an exterior wall and its eaves.

Fire pit A built-in masonry well, typically built into the center of the deck, used to contain a fire. Some portable metal hearths are also called fire pits.

Floodlights Outdoor lights with strong, bright beams used for security or to highlight a large object, such as an arbor or tree.

Fluting A decorative motif consisting of a series of parallel, uniform grooves.

Focal point A design term for the dominant visual element in a space.

Footing A concrete pad, usually at the frost line, that supports posts, piers, or stairs.

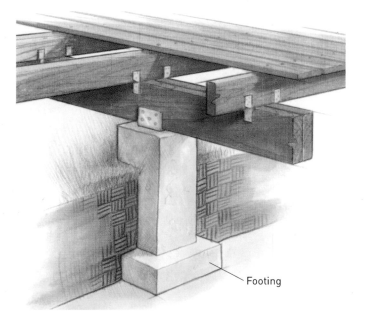

Footing

Frost line The maximum depth at which soil freezes in a given locale. Footings generally must sit below the frost line in colder climates or else heaving, due to water in soil freezing, can cause structural instability.

Gazebo A framed structure with a peaked roof that is usually octagonal. Gazebos offer protection from the rain and sun, and can stand alone or be part of a deck.

Grade The finished level of the ground surrounding a landscaping or construction project. Also, the planned level of the ground around a project that is in progress.

Ground Fault Circuit Interrupter (GFCI) A device that monitors the loss of current in an electrical circuit. If an interruption occurs, the GFCI quickly shuts off current to that circuit. Codes require GFCIs on cir-cuits near water, such as near a spa or ornamental pool.

Guardrail An assembly of posts, balusters (or some other material), and rails that is installed around the edges of a deck for safety.

Handrail A narrow railing at stairs that is designed to be grasped by the hand for support when ascending or descending.

Header joist A building component that's attached to common joists, usually at a right angle, to help hold them in position and to provide rigidity.

Heartwood The older, nonliving central wood of a tree, Usually darker and denser than younger outer layers of the tree (sapwood), heartwood sometimes has decay- and insect-resistant properties.

High Density Polyethylene (HDPE) A petroleum-based dense plastic, often recycled from milk jugs and plastic bags, used to make composite lumber.

Ipe A dense hardwood logged from tropical forests that is naturally resistant to rot, decay, insects, and fire.

Joist A structural member, usually two-by lumber, commonly placed perpendicularly across beams to support deck boards.

Joist hanger A metal framing connector used to join joists to a ledger board and header joists.

Lattice An open framework made of wood, metal, or plastic strips—usually preassembled and typically in a crisscross pattern—that's used to build trellises, privacy and wind screens, and skirting to hide a deck's underside.

Ledger An important structural component used to attach a deck to the side of a house.

Low-voltage lighting Easy-to-install outdoor lighting fixtures that are powered by low-voltage direct current. (Transformers are used to convert 120-volt household current to 15 volts or less.)

Pergola An ornamental, framed structure that is attached on one end to a wall and supported by posts or columns on the other. Pergolas are often used to provide shade on a deck.

Pier A masonry support that rests on a footing and supports a beam.

Pilaster A decorative architectural detail that looks as though it's a rectangular column with a capital and

base but in reality only projects slightly from an exterior wall.

Plan drawing A drawing that shows an overhead view of the deck and specifies dimensions, along with the locations and sizes of components.

Post A vertical member, usually 4x4 or 6x6, that supports a beam or railing.

Pressure-treated lumber Wood that has had preservative forced into it under pressure to make it decay- and insect-resistant.

Proportion The relationship of parts or objects to one another based on their size and commonly accepted rules of what looks pleasing to the eye.

PVC A common thermoplastic resin, frequently called vinyl, used in a wide variety of building products.

Pergola

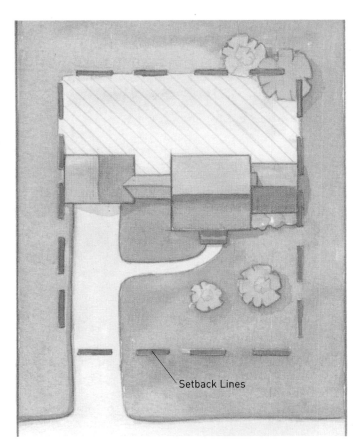

Setback Lines

Railing cap A horizontal piece of lumber laid over the top rail that's often wide enough to set objects on. Railing caps sometimes cover post tops as well.

Riser Vertical boards sometimes placed between stringers and under treads on stairs.

Scale The relationship of a structure or building's size to people, nearby objects, and the surrounding space. Also, the relationship of elements of a structure to the whole.

Sealer A water- or oil-based product applied to deck lumber to prevent moisture penetration and its damaging effects on wood. Also called water repellent.

Setback The legally required distance of a structure or some other feature (a well or a septic system, for ex-

ample) from the property line.

Site plan A drawing that maps out a house and yard. Also called a base plan.

Skirt board Solid band of horizontal wood members installed around the deck perimeter to conceal exposed ends of joists and deck boards.

Skirting Material, generally made of narrow slats or lattice, that covers or screens the space between the edge of the deck and the ground.

Stringer A wide, angled board that supports stair treads and risers.

Synthetic decking Any engineered decking material made from plastics or composites.

Tongue and groove A joint made by fitting a tongue on the edge of a board into a matching groove on the edge of another board.

Tread The board you step on when using stairs.

Trellis A structure designed to support vines that's used for ornamental purposes or to create privacy.

Ultraviolet (UV) light The range of invisible radiation wavelengths, just beyond violet in the visible spectrum, that can be particularly damaging to outdoor wood structures such as decks.

Uplighting A dramatic light treatment whereby a light is placed at the base of an object, pointing upward at it. This is an effective way to highlight trees, plantings, and architectural elements.

Vinyl A shiny, tough, and flexible plastic that is used especially for flooring, siding, decking, and railing. Also called PVC.

Index

Credits

page 1: Brian Vanden Brink, design: Robinson & Grisaru **page 2:** courtesy of Western Red Cedar Lumber Association www.wrcla.org **page 6:** Brian Vanden Brink, design: Mark Hutker **page 7:** *top* courtesy of ShadeScapes USA; *middle* courtesy of CableRail by Feeney Architectural Products © www.cablerail.com 2006, design: Richard Shugar, Eugene, OR; *bottom* courtesy of Sundance Spas **page 8:** Brian Vanden Brink **page 10:** courtesy of the Southern Pine Council, photo: Bruce Nellans, Deer Valley Studios, design: Bruce Pierce, Concepts In Design, Des Moines, IA **page 11:** *top* Crandall and Crandall; *bottom* courtesy of Western Red Cedar Lumber Association www.wrcla.org **pages 12-13:** Brian Vanden Brink, design: Dominic Mercadante **pages 14-15:** Brian Vanden Brink, design: Elliott Elliott Norelius **page 17:** Brian Vanden Brink, design: John Morris **page 18:** courtesy of California Redwood Association, design: Craig Townsend, photo: Marvin Sloben **page 19:** courtesy of Empyrean International **page 20:** courtesy of Western Red Cedar Lumber Association www.wrcla.org **page 21:** Robert Perron, design: Peter Jackson **page 22:** Lucianna Samu **page 23:** courtesy of Andersen Windows, Inc. "Andersen" is a registered trademark of Andersen Corporation. © 2005 Andersen Corporation. All rights reserved. **page 24:** courtesy of Andersen Windows, Inc. "Andersen" is a registered trademark of Andersen Corporation. © 2005 Andersen Corporation. All rights reserved. **page 25:** Brian Vanden Brink, design: Rob Whitten **pages 26-27:** Robert Perron, design: Robert Page **page 28:** *top* courtesy of Summer Classics; *bottom* Brian Vanden Brink, design: Steven Foote **page 29:** Brian Vanden Brink **page 30:** *top* courtesy of Western Red Cedar Lumber Association www.wrcla.org; *bottom* Crandall and Crandall **page 31:** Robert Perron, design: Peter Jackson **page 32:** Robert Perron, design: Robert Page **page 33:** courtesy of TimberTech **pages 34-35:** Lars Dalsgaard **pages 36-37:** courtesy of Wolman **page 38:** courtesy of Veranda **page 39:** Brian Vanden Brink, design: Stephen Blatt **page 40:** Lars Dalsgaard **page 41:** Brian Vanden Brink **pages 42-43:** courtesy of TimberTech **page 44:** courtesy of California Redwood Association, design: Decks by Kiefer, photo: Ernest Braun **page 45:** courtesy of Veranda **page 46:** Treve Johnson **page 47:** *top* courtesy of CableRail by Feeney Architectural Products © www.cablerail.com 2006, design: Scott/Edwards Architecture, Portland, OR; *bottom* courtesy of Weyerhaeuser **page 48:** courtesy of Trex **page 49:** *top* courtesy of California Redwood Association, design: Scott Padgett, photo: Ernest Braun; *bottom* courtesy of Western Red Cedar Lumber Association www.wrcla.org **page 50:** *top* courtesy of Empyrean International; *bottom left & bottom right* courtesy of Western Red Cedar Lumber Association www.wrcla.org **page 51:** courtesy of Empyrean International **pages 52-53:** courtesy of NanaWall Systems, Inc., design: William Duff, WD ARCH, San Francisco, CA, Marina Penthouse, Wood Framed Folding System WD65 Outswing 3L1R **page 54:** courtesy of Andersen Windows, Inc. "Andersen" is a registered trademark of Andersen Corporation. © 2005 Andersen Corporation. All rights reserved. **page 55:** Mark Samu **page 56:** courtesy of Andersen Windows, Inc. "Andersen" is a registered trademark of Andersen Corporation. © 2005 Andersen Corporation. All rights reserved. **page 57:** *top* courtesy of Pella® Windows and Doors; *bottom* Robert Perron, design: Peter Jackson **pages 58-59:** courtesy of NanaWall Systems, Inc. Hilltop Residence, Mill Valley, CA, Wood Framed Individual Panel Sliding System HSW65 Silver Medal, Home Book's Design Excellence Award **page 61:** courtesy of NanaWall Systems, Inc. **page 62:** courtesy of Western Red Cedar Lumber Association www.wrcla.org **page 63:** David Cro, design: Archadeck of North Atlanta **page 64:** courtesy of Western Red Cedar Lumber Association www.wrcla.org **page 65:** *top* courtesy of CableRail by Feeney Architectural Products © www.cablerail.com 2006; *bottom left* Mark Samu; *bottom right* courtesy of California Redwood Association, design: Bowie Gridley Architects, photo: Peter Krogh **page 66:** Mark Samu **page 67:** *top* courtesy of Procell; *bottom* courtesy of CableRail by Feeney Architectural Products © www.cablerail.com 2006; *right* courtesy of Universal Forest Products **pages 68-69:** David Cro, design: Archadeck of North Atlanta **page 70:** Brian Vanden Brink, design: Jack Silverio **page 71:** *left* Lucianna Samu; *right* Jim Westphalen **pages 72-73:** Brian Vanden Brink, design: Jack Silverio **page 74:** Home & Garden Editorial Services **page 75:** *top* courtesy of Western Red Cedar Lumber Association www.wrcla.org; *bottom* courtesy of California Redwood Association, design: Scott Padgett, photo: Ernest Braun **page 76:** courtesy of Trex **page 77:** Crandall and Crandall **page 78:** Brian Vanden Brink **page 79:** *top* Brian Vanden Brink, design: Faesey-Smith; *bottom* courtesy of Punch! Software **page 80:** courtesy of the Southern Pine Council **page 81:** Brian Vanden Brink **page 82:** Robert Perron, design: Robert Page **page 83:** courtesy of California Redwood Association, design: Joseph Wood, photos: Marvin Sloben **page 84:** *left* Brian Vanden Brink, design: Robinson & Grisaru; *right* Robert Perron, design: Paul Bailey **page 85:** courtesy of Weyerhaeuser **page 86:** *top left* courtesy of California Redwood Association, design: Peter Hirano, photo: Tom Rider; *top right* courtesy of Western Red Cedar Lumber Association www.wrcla.org; *bottom* Brian Vanden Brink, design: John Morris **page 87:** Robert Perron **page 88:** *bottom left* courtesy of Deckorators; *center* courtesy of Universal Forest Products **page 89:** *bottom* courtesy of Deckorators; *top right* courtesy of TimberTech **page 90:** *top & bottom left* courtesy of Deckorators; *bottom right* courtesy of Universal Forest Products **page 91:** *top left* courtesy of CableRail by Feeney Architectural Products © www.cablerail.com 2006, design: James Hill Architect, San Francisco, CA; *top right* courtesy of CableRail by Feeney Architectural Products © www.cablerail.com 2006; *bottom* courtesy of Universal Forest Products **page 92:** *top* courtesy of California Redwood Association, design: Alex Porter, photo: Leslie Wright Dow; *bottom* Brian Vanden Brink **page 93:** *top left* courtesy of TimberTech; *top right* courtesy of Trex; *right* David Cro, design: Archadeck of North Atlanta; *bottom* Home & Garden Editorial Services **page 94:** courtesy of Trex **page 95:** *top left* courtesy of Tamko; *top right* courtesy of TimberTech; *bottom* courtesy of Trex **page 96:** courtesy of Cascades **page 97:** *center* courtesy of Tamko; *right* Jessie Walker, design: Ellen Van Buskirk **page 98:** *left* courtesy of Cascades; *bottom left & right* courtesy of Tamko **page 99:** Brian Vanden Brink, design: Stephen Blatt **page 100:** *left* courtesy of Western Red Cedar Lumber Association www.wrcla.org; *right* courtesy of Progress Lighting **page 101:** courtesy of CableRail by Feeney Architectural Products © www.cablerail.com, design: Richard Shugar, Eugene, OR **page 102:** courtesy of Hadco Lighting **page 103:** *top* courtesy of Highpoint Deck Lighting; *bottom* courtesy of Western Red Cedar Lumber Association www.wrcla.org **pages 104-105:** courtesy of Universal Forest Products **page 106:** courtesy of California Redwood Association, design: Gary McCook, photo: Marvin Sloben **page 107:** courtesy of Western Red Cedar Lumber Association www.wrcla.org **page 108:** *top* courtesy of Cecco Trading, Inc.; *bottom* Home & Garden Editorial Services **page 109:** *top* courtesy of Cecco Trading, Inc.; *bottom* Robert Perron, design: Robert Page **page 110:** courtesy of Grace Construction Products **page 111:** *top* courtesy of Timber Treatment Technologies; *bottom* courtesy of the Southern Pine Council **page 112:** courtesy of Trex **page 113:** *top & bottom left* courtesy of Trex; *bottom right* courtesy of Procell **page 114:** courtesy of Royal Crown Ltd. **page 115:** *top* courtesy of Correct Building Products; *bottom* courtesy of Trex **page 116:** courtesy of Cascades **page 117:** courtesy of AridDek **page 118:** Robert Perron, design: Robert Page **page 119:** courtesy of Gaco Western **page 120:** *top* courtesy of California Redwood Association, design: Timothy Bitts, photo: Ernest Braun; *bottom* courtesy of California Redwood Association, design: Scott Padgett, photo: Ernest Braun **page 121:** Brian Vanden Brink **pages 122-123:** Home & Garden Editorial Services **pages 124-125:** Home & Garden Editorial Services **page 126:** courtesy of Tiger Claw **page 127:** courtesy of EB-TY Hidden Deck-Fastening Systems **pages 128-129:** courtesy of Hadco Lighting **page 131:** courtesy of Char-Broil **pages 132-133:** courtesy of Highpoint Deck Lighting **page 134:** *left* courtesy of CableRail by Feeney Architectural Products © www.cablerail.com 2006; *right* courtesy of Trex **page 135:** Crandall and Crandall **page 136:** *top* courtesy of Universal Forest Products; *bottom* courtesy of California Redwood Association, design: Dr. Robert Powers, photo: Ernest Braun **page 137:** *top* courtesy of Western Red Cedar Lumber Association www.wrcla.org; *bottom* Robert Perron **pages 141-142:** courtesy of Trex **pages 143-144:** courtesy of ShadeScapes USA **page 144:** Brian Vanden Brink **page 145:** courtesy of Trex **page 146:** *top* courtesy of Summer Classics; *bottom* courtesy of ShadeScapes USA **page 147:** courtesy of ShadeScapes USA **page 148:** Crandall and Crandall **page 149:** *top* courtesy of Shade Sails; *bottom* courtesy of Gale Pacific **page 150:** Robert Perron **page 151:** David Cro, design: Archadeck of North Atlanta **pages 152-153:** David Cro, design: Archadeck of North Atlanta **page 154:** Crandall and Crandall **page 155:** courtesy of Sundance Spas **pages 156-157:** Lars Dalsgaard **page 159:** courtesy of Summer Classics **page 160:** Robert Perron, design: Rai Muhlbauer **page 161:** Brian Vanden Brink, design: Stanley Tigerman **page 162:** Robert Perron, design: Dan Haslegrave **page 163:** *top* Robert Perron, design: Dan Haslegrave; *bottom* courtesy of Summerwood **pages 164-165:** Brian Vanden Brink, design: Horiuchi & Solien **page 166:** courtesy of Summer Classics **page 167:** *top* Brian Vanden Brink, design: Weatherend Estate Furniture; *bottom* Crandall and Crandall **pages 168-169:** Lars Dalsgaard **page 170:** *top left* Robert Perron, design: Joseph Sepot; *bottom left & right* courtesy of Brookbend **page 171:** Brian Vanden Brink, design: Carol De Tine **page 172:** Lars Dalsgaard **page 173:** Robert Perron, design: Joseph Sepot **page 174:** courtesy of California Redwood Association, design: Mark Allen, photo: Ernest Braun **page 175:** courtesy of TimberTech **page 176:** courtesy of Highpoint Deck Lighting **page 177:** *top left, bottom left & right* courtesy of Highpoint Deck Lighting; *left middle* courtesy of Progress Lighting **page 178:** courtesy of Sundance Spas **page 179:** *top left* courtesy of Western Red Cedar Lumber Association www.wrcla.org; *top right* courtesy of Sundance Spas; *bottom* courtesy of Jacuzzi **page 180:** *top* Brian Vanden Brink, design: Robinson & Grisaru; *bottom* courtesy of Sundance Spas **page 181:** courtesy of Wolman **pages 182-183:** *top* courtesy of Dry-B-Lo; *bottom left* courtesy of Western Red Cedar Lumber Association www.wrcla.org; *bottom right* courtesy of Trex **page 184:** Crandall and Crandall **page 185:** *top* Crandall and Crandall; *bottom* Ken Kelly **page 186:** *left* courtesy of California Redwood Association, design: Timothy Bitts, photo: Ernest Braun; *right* courtesy of Hearth & Home Technologies **page 187:** *top* courtesy of Trex; *bottom* courtesy of Blue Rhino **page 188:** Crandall and Crandall **page 190:** Brian Vanden Brink, design: Design Group Three **page 191:** courtesy of Trex **page 192:** *top* David Cro, design: Archadeck of North Atlanta; *bottom* Crandall and Crandall **page 193:** Brian Vanden Brink, design: Jack Silverio **page 194:** courtesy of Weyerhaeuser **page 195:** *top & middle* courtesy of Weyerhaeuser; *bottom* courtesy of Hooks and Lattice **page 196:** Crandall and Crandall **page 197:** Home & Garden Editorial Services **page 198:** *left* courtesy of Weyerhaeuser; *right* courtesy of California Redwood Association, design: Eli Sutton, photo: Ernest Braun **page 199:** *top* Brian Vanden Brink, design: Rob Whitten; *bottom* courtesy of TimberTech **pages 200-201:** Jim Westphalen, design: Brad Rabinowitz Architects **pages 202-203:** Home & Garden Editorial Services **pages 204-205:** Home & Garden Editorial Services **pages 206-207:** Mike Ortega, design: Adams Architects **pages 208-209:** Brian Vanden Brink, design: Rob Whitten **page 210:** Crandall and Crandall **page 212:** courtesy of California Redwood Association, design: Alex Porter, photo: Leslie Wright Dow **page 213:** Brian Vanden Brink, design: South Mountain Company Builders **pages 214-215:** courtesy of Wolman **pages 216-217:** Mark Samu **pages 218-219:** courtesy of Dry-B-Lo **pages 220-221:** Robert Perron, design: Joseph Sepot **pages 222-223:** Robert Perron, design: Joseph Sepot **page 224:** courtesy of California Redwood Association, design: Gary Papers, photo: Stephen Cridland **page 225:** Robert Perron **pages 226-227:** courtesy of California Redwood Association, design: Scott E. Smith, photo: Ernest Braun **pages 228-229:** courtesy of California Redwood Association, design: Scott Padgett, photos: Ernest Braun **pages 230-231:** courtesy of Western Red Cedar Lumber Association www.wrcla.org **page 232:** Home & Garden Editorial Services **page 233:** Brian Vanden Brink **pages 234-235:** Mark Samu **page 236:** courtesy of Universal Forest Products **page 237:** courtesy of DekBrands **page 238:** courtesy of California Redwood Association, design: Christopher Klos, photo: Ernest Braun **page 239:** Crandall and Crandall **page 285:** Brian Vanden Brink, design: Rob Whitten **page 287:** Brian Vanden Brink, design: Jack Silverio

If you like **1001 Ideas for Decks**

take a look at the rest of the

1001 Ideas series

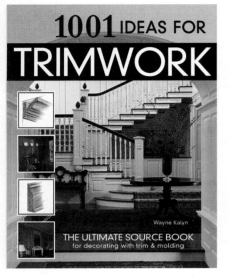

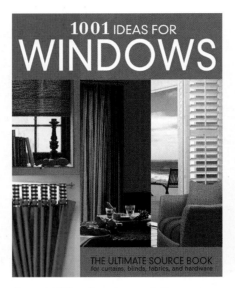

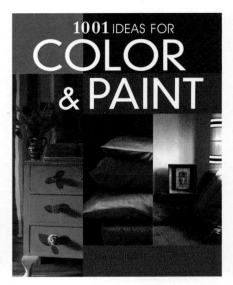

Over 1,000 color photos & illustrations.
ISBN-10: 1-58011-260-9
ISBN-13: 978-1-58011-260-4
CH # 279402
256 pages, 8½" × 10⅞"
$24.95 US / $29.95 CAN

Over 1,000 color photos & illustrations.
ISBN-10: 1-58011-224-2
ISBN-13: 978-1-58011-224-6
CH # 279408
240 pp, 8½" × 10⅞"
$24.95 US / $34.95 CAN

Over 1,000 color photos & illustrations.
ISBN-10: 1-58011-288-9
ISBN-13: 978-1-58011-288-8
CH # 279395
240 pp, 8½" × 10⅞"
$24.95 US / $34.95 CAN

Related Creative Homeowner Titles

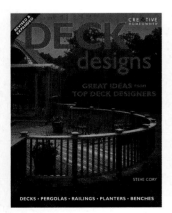

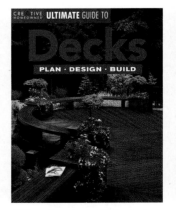

280+ color photos & illustrations.
ISBN-10: 1-58011-269-2
ISBN-13: 978-1-58011-269-7
CH # 277376
224 pp.; 8½" × 10⅞"
$19.95 US / $24.95 CAN

170+ color photos & illustrations.
ISBN-10: 1-58011-147-5
ISBN-13: 978-1-58011-147-8
CH # 277155
128 pp.; 8½" × 10⅞"
$12.95 US / $19.95 CAN

650+ color photos & illustrations.
ISBN-10: 1-58011-148-3
ISBN-13: 978-1-58011-148-5
CH # 277168
288 pp.; 8½" × 10⅞"
$19.95 US / $24.95 CAN

300+ color photos & illustrations.
ISBN-10: 1-58011-080-0
ISBN-13: 978-1-58011-080-8
CH # 277853
224 pp.; 8½" × 10⅞"
$19.95 US / $29.95 CAN

Look for this and other fine **Creative Homeowner books** wherever books are sold.
For more information and to order direct, visit our Web site at
www.creativehomeowner.com